SCRATCH & SOLVE®

ENCYCLOPÆDIA

Britannica®

Arts & Science

Trivia

Raymond Hamel

**PUZZLE
WRIGHT
PRESS**

An imprint of Sterling
Publishing Co., Inc.

www.puzzlewright.com

Puzzlewright Press, the distinctive Puzzlewright Press logo, and Scratch & Solve
are registered trademarks of Sterling Publishing Co., Inc.

2 4 6 8 10 9 7 5 3 1

Published by Sterling Publishing Co., Inc.
387 Park Avenue South, New York, NY 10016
© 2010 by Raymond Hamel
© 2010 Encyclopædia Britannica, Inc.
Britannica, Encyclopædia Britannica, and the Thistle logo
are registered trademarks of Encyclopædia Britannica, Inc.
Distributed in Canada by Sterling Publishing
c/o Canadian Manda Group, 165 Dufferin Street
Toronto, Ontario, Canada M6K 3H6
Distributed in the United Kingdom by GMC Distribution Services
Castle Place, 166 High Street, Lewes, East Sussex, England BN7 1XU
Distributed in Australia by Capricorn Link (Australia) Pty. Ltd.
P.O. Box 704, Windsor, NSW 2756, Australia

Sterling ISBN 978-1-4027-6634-3

For information about custom editions, special sales, premium and
corporate purchases, please contact Sterling Special Sales
Department at 800-805-5489 or specialsales@sterlingpublishing.com.

CONTENTS

INTRODUCTION

Each trivia question in this book has four answer choices. Scratch the silver circle next to the answer you believe is correct. If you are right, it will say "+10" and you will earn 10 points. If you are wrong, it will show a negative number from –2 to –5, and you will need to pick again. Keep trying until you choose the correct answer. Once you successfully find the correct answer, subtract the scores for the wrong answers from 10 to get your score for that question. For example, if it takes you three tries, and you uncover a –3 and –4 before finding the +10, your score is 10 minus 3 minus 4, for a total of 3 points. The three wrong answers' numbers always total –10, so if you don't find the correct answer until the fourth try, you score zero for that question.

If you score 5000 or more points total, you're a trivia master; keep it up and maybe one day you'll merit your own *Encyclopædia Britannica* entry!

If you score from 3800 to 4999 points, you've clearly got a bookshelf's worth of knowledge in your head!

If you score from 2400 to 3799 points, you might want to do some studying, but you're still more than just a footnote in the history of trivia.

If you score fewer than 2400 points, console yourself by remembering that the definition of trivia is "unimportant things."

What temperature-measuring device consists of two wires of different metals joined at each end?

Pyrometer ⬤ ⬤ Autoclave

Thermocouple ⬤ ⬤ Accelerometer

Which insect needs the proteins found in blood to mature its eggs?

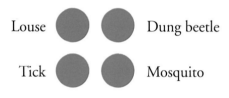

Louse ⬤ ⬤ Dung beetle

Tick ⬤ ⬤ Mosquito

Rocker Roger Daltrey often dressed in clothes made out of the Union Jack while fronting what British band in the 1960s?

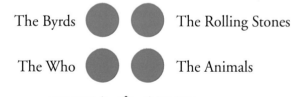

The Byrds ⬤ ⬤ The Rolling Stones

The Who ⬤ ⬤ The Animals

In which year will Halley's Comet make its next visit to Earth as it orbits our Sun?

2031 ⬤ ⬤ 2051

2041 ⬤ ⬤ 2061

What science typically involves control and communication in living organisms, machines, and organizations?

Bistromatics   Positronics

Nutrimatics   Cybernetics

The name of what herb, long associated with Mediterranean cooking, comes from Greek words translating as "mountain joy"?

Saffron   Chamomile

Oregano   Tarragon

What does the first "M" stand for in the name of the MMPI personality test?

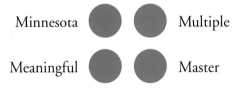

Minnesota   Multiple

Meaningful   Master

The Horsehead Nebula is a cloud of gas and matter situated in what constellation?

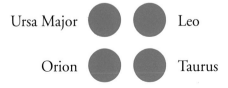

Ursa Major   Leo

Orion   Taurus

Sarsen stones and bluestones were used in the design of which ancient structure?

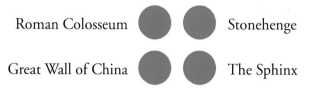

Roman Colosseum   Stonehenge

Great Wall of China   The Sphinx

How many valves are on a standard flügelhorn?

0   5

3   6

The innermost and smallest of the five major moons of Uranus was named after which character from the Shakespeare play *The Tempest*?

Ceres   Miranda

Juno   Claribel

Who was the first woman to have a million-selling country music hit song with her 1935 recording of "I Want to Be a Cowboy's Sweetheart"?

Patsy Montana   Jennie Bowman

Maybelle Carter   Cindy Walker

Burial at Ornans, a huge representation of a peasant funeral containing more than 40 life-size figures, was painted by what advocate of Realism?

Pierre Bonnard 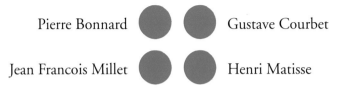 Gustave Courbet

Jean Francois Millet Henri Matisse

Which dramatist's last play, *Déjàvu*, was a sequel to his earlier *Look Back in Anger*, revisiting the main character Jimmy Porter after a 35-year interval?

George Bernard Shaw 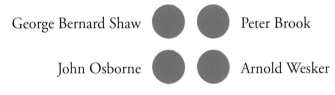 Peter Brook

John Osborne Arnold Wesker

Which astronaut became the second American to orbit the Earth as he flew aboard Aurora 7?

Donald Slayton 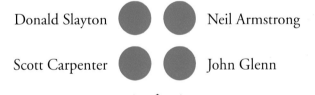 Neil Armstrong

Scott Carpenter John Glenn

Which disco diva's hit songs include "Love to Love You Baby," "Bad Girls," and "She Works Hard for the Money"?

Donna Summer  Chaka Khan

Laura Branigan Gloria Gaynor

Which style of jazz music was popularized in the 1930s by artists such as saxophonist Lester Young and pianist-bandleader Count Basie?

Kansas City   West Coast

Dixieland   Chicago

Who played the sheriff in pursuit of John Rambo in *First Blood*?

Jim Davis   Brian Dennehy

Clint Eastwood   James Woods

Who wrote the Fifth Dimension's hit songs "Wedding Bell Blues" and "Stoned Soul Picnic"?

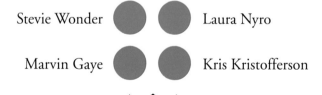

Stevie Wonder   Laura Nyro

Marvin Gaye   Kris Kristofferson

John Backus led a team of 10 IBM employees to create which computer language debuting in 1957 that combined a form of English shorthand with algebraic equations?

Fortran   BASIC

COBOL   Pascal

Which British performer cowrote and directed *Stop the World—I Want to Get Off* in 1961, which gave him his signature songs "What Kind of Fool Am I?" and "Once in a Lifetime"?

Jacques Brel   Anthony Newley

Rex Harrison   Ian Whitcomb

In science, whose principle states that a body immersed in a fluid is acted upon by a buoyant force equal to the weight of the displaced fluid?

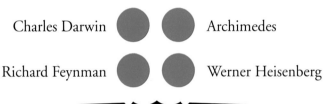

Charles Darwin   Archimedes

Richard Feynman   Werner Heisenberg

In 2005, Marin Alsop become the first woman to be named the musical director of a major American orchestra. Which city's orchestra was it?

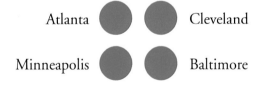

Atlanta   Cleveland

Minneapolis   Baltimore

Which of these rocks is *not* a form of sandstone?

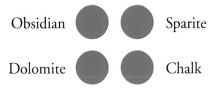

Obsidian   Sparite

Dolomite   Chalk

What does the "R" stand for in the medical diagnostic tool commonly called the MRI?

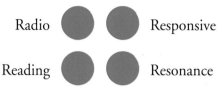

Radio   Responsive

Reading   Resonance

Who created the *Sandman* comic book series for DC Comics and the *Marvel 1602* limited series for Marvel Comics?

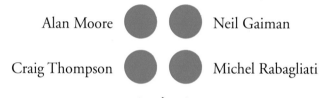

Alan Moore   Neil Gaiman

Craig Thompson   Michel Rabagliati

Which actor-director fulfilled a personal mission by bringing *The Passion of the Christ* to the screen in 2004?

Kevin Costner   John Cassavetes

Sam Shepard   Mel Gibson

Zoo specimens of which bird, that gets its pink color from food containing carotenoid pigments, fade in color if not periodically fed food coloring?

Pelican   Egret

Flamingo   Cockatoo

What canceled NASA program had been scheduled as a successor to the space shuttle program, with plans to carry astronauts to the International Space Station beginning in 2015 and to Mars in 2020?

Cosmos   Constellation

Neptune   Aphrodite

The houbara bustard in Asia is a favorite prey in which type of hunting?

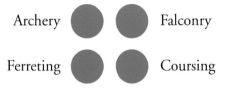

Archery   Falconry

Ferreting   Coursing

Peter Gunn star Craig Stevens made his final film appearance in which movie directed by Blake Edwards?

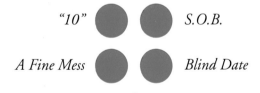

"10"   *S.O.B.*

A Fine Mess   *Blind Date*

The 1925 tone poem *Tapiola* turned out to be the last major work from which composer before he entered a 30-year period of silence at the end of his life?

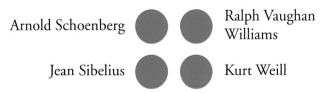

Arnold Schoenberg   Ralph Vaughan Williams

Jean Sibelius   Kurt Weill

Which kind of nut comes from deciduous trees in the genus *Juglans*?

Walnut Peanut

Brazil nut Pistachio

What country singer, born Virginia Patterson Hensley, was killed at age 30 in a plane crash in 1963?

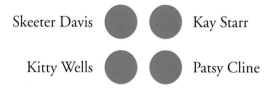

Skeeter Davis Kay Starr

Kitty Wells Patsy Cline

Which part of the face is controlled by the levator anguli oris muscle?

Eyelid Mouth

Nose Forehead

More than half of all bird species can be classified as passerines. What basic characteristic do all passerines possess?

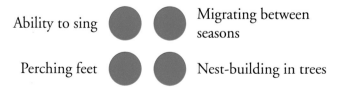

Ability to sing Migrating between seasons

Perching feet Nest-building in trees

Which astronaut circled the Earth 22 times in the space capsule Faith 7, completing the longest and last of the Mercury manned spaceflights?

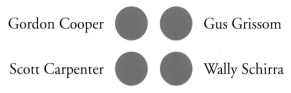

Gordon Cooper

Gus Grissom

Scott Carpenter

Wally Schirra

What noted scientist won a Pulitzer Prize in 1978 for *The Dragons of Eden: Speculations on the Evolution of Human Intelligence* and also wrote the sci-fi novel *Contact*?

Rene Dubos

Carl Sagan

C.P. Snow

Roger Revelle

Ultraviolet radiation from the sun stimulates the production of which vitamin in human skin?

B_1

D

C

K

Ferdinand, the king of Navarre, and three of his noblemen—Berowne, Longaville, and Dumaine—engage in a battle of wits with female counterparts in which Shakespeare play?

Love's Labour's Lost

Macbeth

A Midsummer Night's Dream

The Taming of the Shrew

15

Regulus is the brightest star in which constellation of the Zodiac?

Cancer   Sagittarius

Taurus   Leo

What term is used by engineers to describe a computer system made up of poorly matched components?

Hack   Wiki

Kludge   Bad apple

Hugo de Vries, William Bateson, and Thomas Hunt Morgan were experts in what field of science?

Psychology   Nanotechnology

Marine biology   Genetics

Which of these popular stage musicals was *not* the work of collaborators Fred Ebb and John Kander?

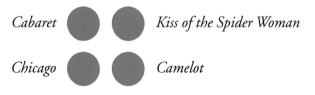

Cabaret   *Kiss of the Spider Woman*

Chicago   *Camelot*

Which architect experimented in the design of two popular lines of corrugated cardboard furniture, Easy Edges (1969–73) and Experimental Edges (1979–82)?

Eileen Gray 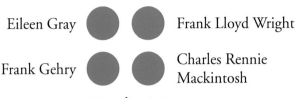 Frank Lloyd Wright

Frank Gehry Charles Rennie Mackintosh

Which composer was unable to write music, or even speak, during the final five years of his life due to aphasia?

Wolfgang Amadeus Mozart 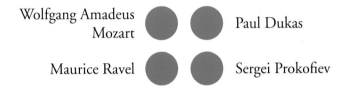 Paul Dukas

Maurice Ravel Sergei Prokofiev

Romanian composer Georges Enesco was also a virtuoso on which musical instrument?

Bassoon  Violin

Flute Piano

Which unit in the meter-kilogram-second system is used to measure electric potential?

Watt 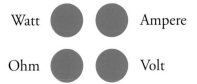 Ampere

Ohm Volt

Which gas was first identified by Scottish botanist Daniel Rutherford in 1772, and first identified as an element by Antoine-Laurent Lavoisier?

Neon   Hydrogen

Nitrogen   Oxygen

A castle in what Danish seaport is the setting for the Shakespeare play *Hamlet*?

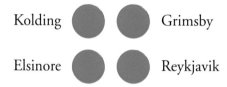

Kolding   Grimsby

Elsinore   Reykjavik

Which architect's most famous work is the Basilica of the Assumption of the Blessed Virgin Mary, the 19th-century Roman Catholic cathedral of Baltimore?

Benjamin Latrobe   Elliott Woods

David Lynn   Charles Bulfinch

What is the largest natural satellite in the solar system?

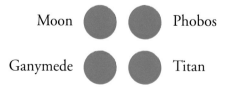

Moon   Phobos

Ganymede   Titan

The Scottish physician Sir James Simpson was the first to use which substance as an anesthetic in 1847?

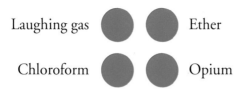

Laughing gas · Ether

Chloroform · Opium

A mealworm is actually the larva of which type of insect?

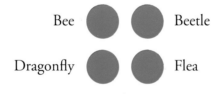

Bee · Beetle

Dragonfly · Flea

Which science was founded upon the principles of uniformitarianism originated by James Hutton?

Geology · Chemistry

Limnology · Meteorology

The phenomenon of photoelectric effect instigated questions about the nature of light-particle vs. wavelike behavior that were finally resolved by which scientist in 1905?

Albert Einstein · Niels Bohr

Enrico Fermi · Marie Curie

The name of which mineral, and birthstone, is derived from the Greek for "not intoxicated," expressing the ancient folk belief that the stone protects its owner against drunkenness?

Onyx ⬤ ⬤ Peridot

Garnet ⬤ ⬤ Amethyst

Which U.S. state was struck in 1964 by an earthquake with a Richter scale magnitude of 9.2, releasing twice as much energy as the San Francisco earthquake of 1906?

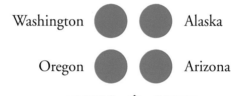

Washington ⬤ ⬤ Alaska

Oregon ⬤ ⬤ Arizona

What is stored in a Leyden jar?

Cheese ⬤ ⬤ Liquid nitrogen

Static electricity ⬤ ⬤ Acid

The original design of which medical instrument consisted of a hollow tube of wood that was 1.5 inches in diameter and 10 inches long, transmitting sound to the ear?

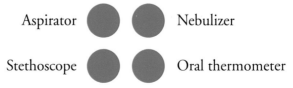

Aspirator ⬤ ⬤ Nebulizer

Stethoscope ⬤ ⬤ Oral thermometer

What device is employed to raise the voltage from electric generators so that electric power can be transmitted over long distances?

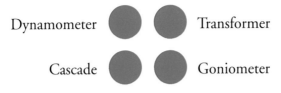

Dynamometer

Transformer

Cascade

Goniometer

What hypothetical atomic particle endows all other particles with mass?

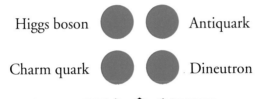

Higgs boson

Antiquark

Charm quark

Dineutron

Which insect has been affected by a mysterious affliction called colony collapse disorder, or CCD, first reported in 2006?

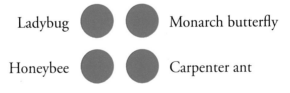

Ladybug

Monarch butterfly

Honeybee

Carpenter ant

The main feature of what type of microscope is that only what is in focus is detected, and anything out of focus appears as black?

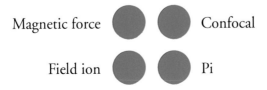

Magnetic force

Confocal

Field ion

Pi

Which British actor won a Tony Award for his performance as Henry VIII in *Anne of the Thousand Days* in 1949?

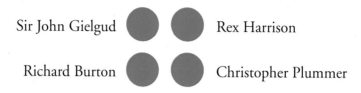

Sir John Gielgud   Rex Harrison

Richard Burton   Christopher Plummer

In physics, what term is given to the conversion of a substance from the solid to the vapor state without its becoming liquid?

Vaporization   Sublimation

Deposition   Evaporation

What is the most common liquid used in a barometer?

Sugar water   Ethyl alcohol

Gasoline   Mercury

The myocardium, pericardium, and endocardium are layers of tissue in which human organ?

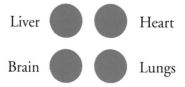

Liver   Heart

Brain   Lungs

Wavelength is usually denoted by which Greek letter?

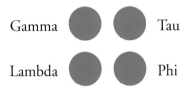

Gamma   Tau

Lambda   Phi

The pH value of a liquid, measuring its acidity or basicity, occurs on a scale of 0 to what maximum value?

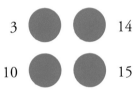

3   14

10   15

Which type of virus carries its genetic blueprint in the form of ribonucleic acid (RNA)?

Rhinovirus   Haplovirus

Echovirus   Retrovirus

The carapace and plastron are bony structures that usually join one another creating a rigid skeletal structure around which animal?

Sponge   Starfish

Turtle   Snail

During the Middle Ages, the bubonic plague was referred to as the "black plague." In this same time period, which disease was called the "white plague"?

Tuberculosis 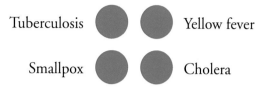 Yellow fever

Smallpox Cholera

Which term was coined by Peter Karlson and Martin Luscher to describe chemicals used to communicate between individuals of the same species?

Hormones 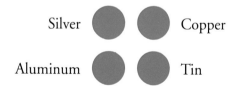 Pheromones

Pyrophorous Oleum

Acanthite is the most important ore containing which metal?

Silver  Copper

Aluminum Tin

Surrealist painter René Magritte was born and died in which country?

Switzerland 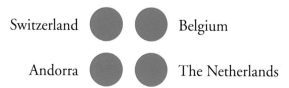 Belgium

Andorra The Netherlands

Which painter worked as a tax collector in the Paris toll office, from which came the nickname by which he was well known in later years, le Douanier ("the Customs Officer")?

Horace Pippin  Piet Mondrian

Pablo Picasso Henri Rousseau

In the language of Esperanto, all singular nouns end in what letter?

G  S

O Y

Beach Boys leader Brian Wilson cowrote many hit songs for Jan and Dean. Which was the only one to reach #1?

"Sidewalk Surfin'" 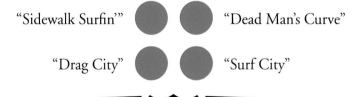 "Dead Man's Curve"

"Drag City" "Surf City"

The "Nine Old Men" were artists who made which studio the leader of film cartoons with their animation of classic features and shorts?

Warner Brothers 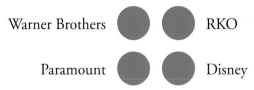 RKO

Paramount Disney

Sir Frank Whittle and Hans Pabst von Ohain were pioneers of which invention?

FM radio   Radar

Jet engine   Television

During the Scopes "Monkey Trial" in Tennessee in 1925, William Jennings Bryan led for the prosecution. Which noted attorney led the defense?

Marcus Garvey   Clarence Darrow

Daniel Webster   Emory Buckner

Which of the following is *not* considered a rare-earth chemical element?

Ytterbium   Lutetium

Lithium   Scandium

Which country singer, born Harold Lloyd Jenkins, created his professional name by merging the names of towns in Arkansas and Texas?

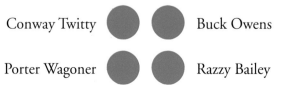

Conway Twitty   Buck Owens

Porter Wagoner   Razzy Bailey

The original Stax and Sun Records recording studios were located in what city?

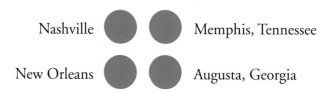

Nashville   Memphis, Tennessee

New Orleans   Augusta, Georgia

Which of the following elements is *not* in Group 1 of the periodic table?

Helium   Cesium

Potassium   Sodium

Which Charles Dickens character has lent his or her name to a variety of trout?

Charles Darnay   Nicholas Nickleby

Dolly Varden   Solomon Pell

What master of Spanish painting was born Doménikos Theotokópoulos?

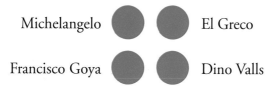

Michelangelo   El Greco

Francisco Goya   Dino Valls

Of which bird are the males called cobs and the females called pens?

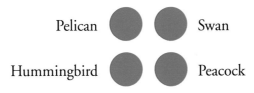

Pelican   Swan

Hummingbird   Peacock

The constellation of Cassiopeia appears roughly in the shape of which letter of the alphabet?

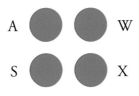

A   W

S   X

The quantity of air taken in with each breath during the respiratory cycle is referred to as what kind of volume?

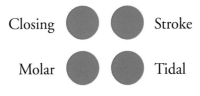

Closing   Stroke

Molar   Tidal

The Schick test is a method for determining susceptibility to which acute disease?

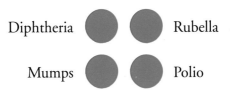

Diphtheria   Rubella

Mumps   Polio

Which amino acid is used by the human body to manufacture the neurotransmitter serotonin and the vitamin niacin?

Tryptophan 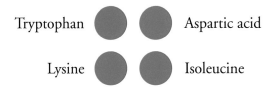 Aspartic acid

Lysine Isoleucine

Which singer burst onto the American scene in 1960 when he played Sir Lancelot in the original Broadway production of *Camelot*?

Engelbert Humperdinck 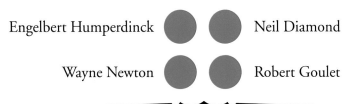 Neil Diamond

Wayne Newton Robert Goulet

What was the name of Samantha's identical-looking cousin on the sitcom *Bewitched*?

Sarah  Sissy

Serena Samara

Gregor Mendel performed his pioneering experimental program in hybridization using which vegetable?

Radish 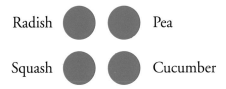 Pea

Squash Cucumber

Which actor played the male lead opposite Jennifer Jones in *Duel in the Sun* (1946) and *Portrait of Jennie* (1948)?

Gary Cooper   Joseph Cotten

Burt Lancaster   Gregory Peck

"Slippery When Wet," "Too Hot ta Trot," and "Still" were #1 songs for what vocal group?

The Silhouettes   The Platters

The Five Keys   The Commodores

Which physicist, at age 18 the youngest member of the Manhattan Project team, was later found to have sent top-secret information to Moscow contacts, facilitating Soviet development of the atomic bomb?

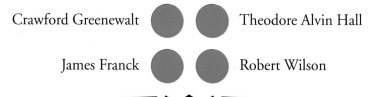

Crawford Greenewalt   Theodore Alvin Hall

James Franck   Robert Wilson

Which actor appeared with his first wife in the movie *Shanghai Surprise* and with his second wife in *She's So Lovely*?

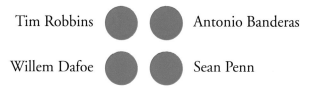

Tim Robbins   Antonio Banderas

Willem Dafoe   Sean Penn

Which German physicist discovered a way to formulate quantum mechanics in terms of matrices in 1925, and was awarded the Nobel Prize for Physics for 1932?

James Franck 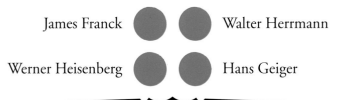 Walter Herrmann

Werner Heisenberg Hans Geiger

Which American was the designer of SpaceShipOne in 2004, the first private manned spacecraft?

Gary Kitmacher 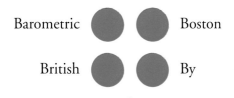 Burt Rutan

David Lindsay Eugene Lally

A BTU is a specific measure of heat. What does the B in BTU stand for?

Barometric 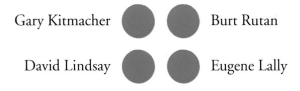 Boston

British By

One horsepower will lift how many pounds a distance of one foot in one minute?

100 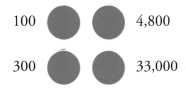 4,800

300 33,000

The typical human being has how many pairs of chromosomes?

13  23

19 39

Enceladus is the brightest of all moons orbiting which planet?

Mars  Saturn

Jupiter Uranus

Which variety of cream contains the highest percentage of butterfat?

Half and half 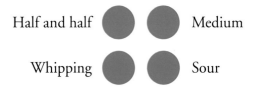 Medium

Whipping Sour

Which guitarist was a member of the groups the Yardbirds, John Mayall's Bluesbreakers, and Cream?

Jimi Hendrix  Eric Clapton

Carlos Santana Jeff Beck

What is traditionally the name of the dog in Punch-and-Judy plays?

Jonesy   Toby

Hector   Samuel

Who starred as young navy officer candidate Zack Mayo in the 1982 movie *An Officer and a Gentleman*?

Tom Cruise   Richard Gere

Beau Bridges   Martin Sheen

In the U.S., a bushel is made up of 32 dry quarts, equivalent to how many pecks?

4   6

5   8

Which element combines with iron to make the mineral iron pyrite?

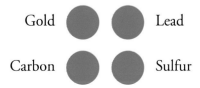

Gold   Lead

Carbon   Sulfur

What system of musical notation is based on a player's finger positions rather than notes showing rhythm and pitch?

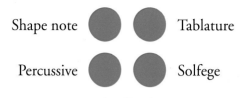

Shape note   Tablature

Percussive   Solfege

British painter George Stubbs spent a period of 18 months studying the anatomy of what animal, out of which came a major work of reference for naturalists and artists alike?

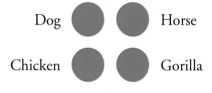

Dog   Horse

Chicken   Gorilla

The hormone melatonin plays an important role in the regulation of sleep cycles in humans. It is secreted by which gland?

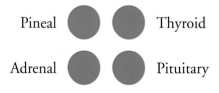

Pineal   Thyroid

Adrenal   Pituitary

The official unit for radioactivity in the International System of Units is named after what Nobel Prize–winning physicist?

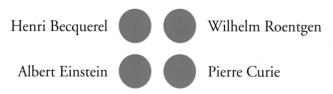

Henri Becquerel   Wilhelm Roentgen

Albert Einstein   Pierre Curie

Which is the largest of the nonhuman primates native to South America?

Squirrel monkey 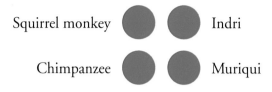 Indri

Chimpanzee Muriqui

Which of the following is *not* one of the nonmetallic elements found in the halogen group?

Sodium  Fluorine

Iodine Bromine

What dwarf planet and largest known asteroid in the asteroid belt was the first asteroid to be discovered, in 1801?

Ceres  Juno

Vesta Galileo

Who composed "Gott erhalte Franz den Kaiser" ("God Save Emperor Francis"), once Austria's national anthem, revisiting the song as a theme for variations in one of his finest string quartets, the *Emperor Quartet*?

Johann Sebastian Bach 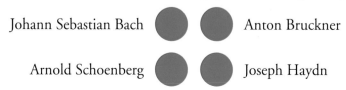 Anton Bruckner

Arnold Schoenberg Joseph Haydn

Which of these mammals has the longest gestation period?

Human   Elephant

Giraffe   Grizzly bear

According the standard model of particle physics, how many fundamental particles make up the basic ingredients of the universe?

3   6

4   12

Which of these observatories operates from the surface of Earth, rather than aboard an orbiting satellite?

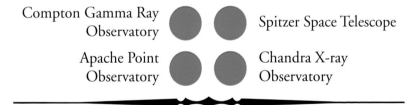

Compton Gamma Ray
Observatory   Spitzer Space Telescope

Apache Point
Observatory   Chandra X-ray
Observatory

Which band leader helped squares learn to be hep with his "Hepsters Dictionary" and "Swingformation Bureau" booklets?

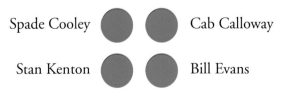

Spade Cooley   Cab Calloway

Stan Kenton   Bill Evans

Conductor Eugene Ormandy, film director Michael Curtiz, and nuclear physicist Edward Teller were all born in which country?

Hungary   Slovenia

Serbia   Romania

Who set the world's landplane speed record in 1935; lowered the transcontinental flight time record to 7 hours, 28 minutes in 1937; and circled the Earth in record time in 1938?

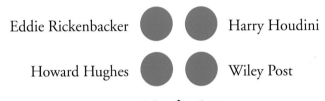

Eddie Rickenbacker   Harry Houdini

Howard Hughes   Wiley Post

Jazz artist Pee Wee Russell was a distinctive stylist on what musical instrument?

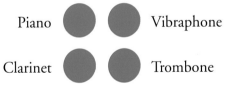

Piano   Vibraphone

Clarinet   Trombone

16th-century Venetian painter Tiziano Vecellio was known as Titian, and Paolo Caliari was known as Paolo Veronese. By which name was Jacopo Robusti known?

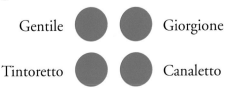

Gentile   Giorgione

Tintoretto   Canaletto

Which breed of terrier greatly resembles a lamb?

Tibetan 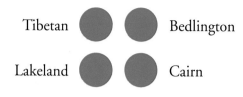 Bedlington

Lakeland Cairn

Which teen idol recorded the #1 songs "Venus" (1959) and "Why" (1960)?

Frankie Avalon 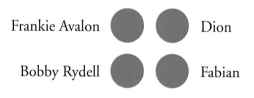 Dion

Bobby Rydell Fabian

Russian physiologist Ivan Pavlov was known chiefly for his work on the conditioned reflex, employing mental conditioning associated with hunger in which animal?

Cat  Monkey

Horse Dog

Who was the subject of a 1950s ballet by Aram Khachaturian and a 1960 film starring Kirk Douglas?

Vincent Van Gogh 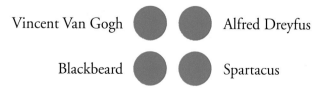 Alfred Dreyfus

Blackbeard Spartacus

Which chemical element imparts a lavender color to a flame, has a green vapor, and is the seventh most abundant element in Earth's crust?

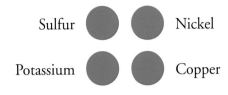

Sulfur

Nickel

Potassium

Copper

Which of these food fish is a flatfish?

Tilapia

Tilefish

Grouper

Turbot

What color was the hat worn by the title character in Disney's *Pinocchio*?

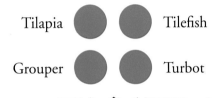

Red

Green

Yellow

Blue

Which chemical element was named after the Greek word for "lazy," because of its chemical inertness?

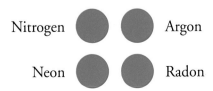

Nitrogen

Argon

Neon

Radon

Which variety of cheese is sprayed with spores of penicillium candidum, a mold that forms a thin, downy white crust?

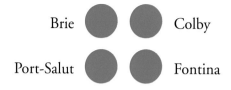

Brie   Colby

Port-Salut   Fontina

Which Iowa city is where Frederick L. Maytag invented a "hand power" washing machine (1907) and his motor-driven washer (1911), and is also noted as the home of Maytag blue cheese?

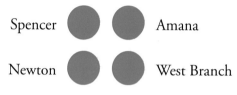

Spencer   Amana

Newton   West Branch

Which of these Apple innovations was the first introduced?

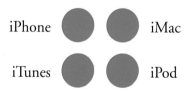

iPhone   iMac

iTunes   iPod

How many different unique arrangements can be made of the 5 squares in the figures called pentominoes?

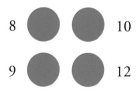

8   10

9   12

Which artist had to flee Rome in 1606 after he killed one Ranuccio Tomassoni during a furious brawl over a disputed score in a game of tennis?

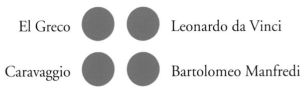

El Greco   Leonardo da Vinci

Caravaggio   Bartolomeo Manfredi

In physics, which name is given to a quantity that has both magnitude and direction?

Affinity   Vector

Tensor   Array

Which part of a building may be described as a mansard?

Window   Stairway

Roof   Wall

What may be measured using the Mercalli scale?

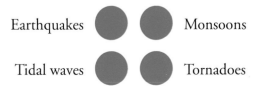

Earthquakes   Monsoons

Tidal waves   Tornadoes

At room temperature, what color is the chemical element iodine?

Red   Green

Yellow   Black

Which computer operating system was created in the early 1990s by Finnish software engineer Linus Torvalds and the Free Software Foundation?

OS   Linux

Android   MS-DOS

Which actress earned an Academy Award nomination for Best Supporting Actress playing Jane Fonda's fun-loving mother in *Barefoot in the Park*?

Helen Hayes   Vanessa Redgrave

Mildred Natwick   Thelma Ritter

The New Madrid Fault, a deep-seated fracture in the Earth's crust and cause of 8.0-magnitude earthquakes in 1811 and 1812, is located in which country?

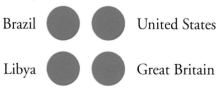

Brazil   United States

Libya   Great Britain

Which metal makes up about 90% of the composition of modern pewter?

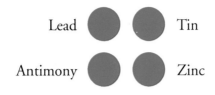

Lead   Tin

Antimony   Zinc

In which part of the body is the sciatic nerve located?

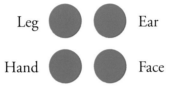

Leg   Ear

Hand   Face

What IBM computer was the first machine to win a chess game against a reigning world champion (Garry Kasparov) under regular time controls?

Deep Blue   Big Blue

Deep Thought   Chessmaster 3000

Which artist's *The Wedding of Samson* (1638) can be seen as an attempt to create a much livelier composition of characters than Leonardo da Vinci had achieved in his *Last Supper*?

Donatello   El Greco

Caravaggio   Rembrandt

The world's highest volcano is a part of which mountain range?

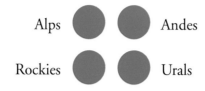

Alps   Andes

Rockies   Urals

Jane Goodall is best known for her long-term research on the behavior of chimpanzees at the Gombe Stream National Park in which African nation?

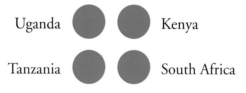

Uganda   Kenya

Tanzania   South Africa

What egg-laying mammal found in Australia bears a great resemblance to the unrelated hedgehog?

Bilby   Dunnart

Echidna   Melomys

Which sculptor is best remembered for his *Greek Slave* (1843), a white marble statue of a nude girl in chains that loosely bind her hands in front of her?

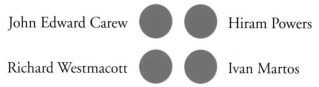

John Edward Carew   Hiram Powers

Richard Westmacott   Ivan Martos

The nephron is a structure in which organ that produces urine in the process of removing waste and excess substances from the blood?

Brain   Pancreas

Liver   Kidney

Whose discovery of nuclear fission, finding that uranium bombarded by neutrons divided into lighter elements, won him the 1944 Nobel Prize for Chemistry?

Enrico Fermi   Otto Hahn

Albert Einstein   Leo Szilard

Army pathologist Walter Reed demonstrated in 1900 that which disease was transmitted by mosquitoes?

Influenza   Yellow fever

Dengue fever   Malaria

What domed building in Rome, begun in 27 B.C. by the statesman Marcus Vipsanius Agrippa, was dedicated in A.D. 609 as the Church of Santa Maria Rotonda, or Santa Maria ad Martyres?

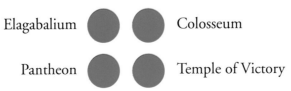

Elagabalium   Colosseum

Pantheon   Temple of Victory

Which percussion instrument is prominent in Franz Liszt's *Piano Concerto No. 1*, where it is used as a solo instrument in the second movement?

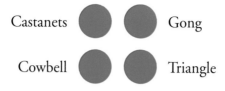

Castanets ⬤ ⬤ Gong

Cowbell ⬤ ⬤ Triangle

Who received patent #174,465 for the development of a device to transmit speech sounds over electric wires, often said to be the most valuable patent ever issued?

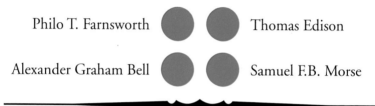

Philo T. Farnsworth ⬤ ⬤ Thomas Edison

Alexander Graham Bell ⬤ ⬤ Samuel F.B. Morse

British physicist James Chadwick was awarded the Nobel Prize for Physics in 1935 for his discovery of which subatomic particle?

Electron ⬤ ⬤ Neutron

Quark ⬤ ⬤ Proton

Which American bandleader and vibraphone player was nicknamed the "King of Mambo"?

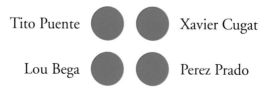

Tito Puente ⬤ ⬤ Xavier Cugat

Lou Bega ⬤ ⬤ Perez Prado

Which film was the last collaboration of Cary Grant and Alfred Hitchcock?

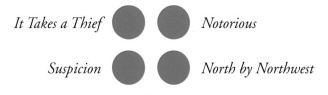

It Takes a Thief   Notorious

Suspicion   North by Northwest

Which is the only one of the halogen elements that is a liquid at room temperature?

Fluorine   Astatine

Bromine   Iodine

Which spice comes from grinding up the dried pods of the shrub *Capsicum annuum*?

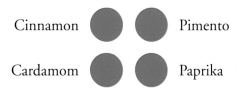

Cinnamon   Pimento

Cardamom   Paprika

The introduction of which animal to Australia in 1859 has led to widespread damage to crops and decreases in the population of native Australian flora and fauna that compete for the same natural resources?

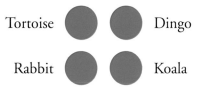

Tortoise   Dingo

Rabbit   Koala

How many pairs of legs does a lobster have?

2   4

3   5

Which part of a plant is most influenced by positive geotropism?

Roots   Fruit

Seeds   Leaves

Which of these is *not* a classification for the body shape of human beings known as a somatotype?

Ectomorph   Neomorph

Mesomorph   Endomorph

After diamond, which mineral is the hardest known natural substance?

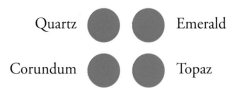

Quartz   Emerald

Corundum   Topaz

Miohippus and *Merychippus* are extinct genera, and ancestors, of which modern animal?

Pig   Horse

Deer   Elephant

The Theseum and the Parthenon, both temples in Athens, are examples of which classic order of architecture?

Roman   Doric

Ionic   Corinthian

The largest extant lizard, the Komodo dragon, is native to which country?

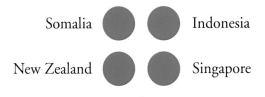

Somalia   Indonesia

New Zealand   Singapore

Which chemical element combines with sulfur to form the orangish mineral realgar?

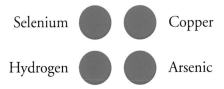

Selenium   Copper

Hydrogen   Arsenic

The tango first appeared around 1880, and by 1915 was a craze in fashionable European circles. In which country did this dance originate?

Argentina ○ ○ Brazil

Spain ○ ○ Portugal

As much as 20% of the world's production of which metal is produced from mines on the rim of the Sudbury basin in Ontario, Canada?

Zinc ○ ○ Nickel

Copper ○ ○ Iron

Which bird comes in such varieties as chinstrap, macaroni, and fairy?

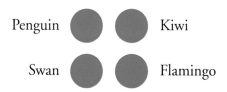

Penguin ○ ○ Kiwi

Swan ○ ○ Flamingo

Which composer's largest choral work is the *War Requiem* for choir and orchestra, based on the Latin requiem mass text and the poems of Wilfred Owen, who was killed in World War I?

Gustav Holst ○ ○ Ralph Vaughan Williams

Hector Berlioz ○ ○ Benjamin Britten

The quince, a fruit popular in jellies and preserves, grows on a tree that is a member of what family?

Apple   Rose

Cherry   Durian

Which of these animals could be described as canine?

Fennec   Vervet

Civet   Margay

Who was the author of the popular self-help book *How to Win Friends and Influence People*?

Leo Buscaglia   Thomas Harris

Werner Erhard   Dale Carnegie

John, Herbert, Harry, and Donald were members of which family musical group out of Piqua, Ohio?

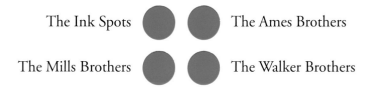

The Ink Spots   The Ames Brothers

The Mills Brothers   The Walker Brothers

Which Italian composer had a contentious relationship with Mozart in the Peter Shaffer play (and film) *Amadeus*?

Antonio Salieri   Vincenzo Bellini

Giuseppe Verdi   Niccolò Paganini

Which stone, a supposed relic of a 14th-century Scandinavian exploration of North America, is housed in a museum in Alexandria, Minnesota, while a 26-ton replica stands in nearby Runestone Park?

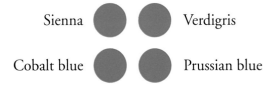

Kensington Stone   Durell Stone

Rosetta Stone   Blarney Stone

Which common pigment is created by mixing copper acetate with vinegar?

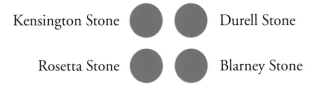

Sienna   Verdigris

Cobalt blue   Prussian blue

What color are the berries produced by the bilberry or whortleberry shrubs?

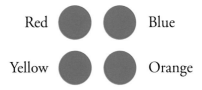

Red   Blue

Yellow   Orange

Wormwood is the primary flavoring ingredient in which drink marketed with an alcohol content of 68 percent by volume?

Absinthe   Campari

Fenny   Aquavit

What was the subject of *The Hite Report*, published in 1976?

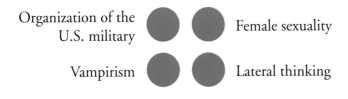

Organization of the U.S. military   Female sexuality

Vampirism   Lateral thinking

Which cosmonaut was the first person to perform a space walk, and later served as the commander of the Soviet Soyuz craft that linked in orbit with the U.S. Apollo craft on July 17, 1975?

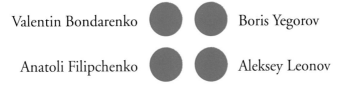

Valentin Bondarenko   Boris Yegorov

Anatoli Filipchenko   Aleksey Leonov

Which architect designed the Woolworth Building in New York City and the United States Supreme Court Building in Washington, D.C.?

Cass Gilbert   Andrew Ellicott

Robert Mills   William Welles Bosworth

What are the food additives sorbitol and acesulfame K used as?

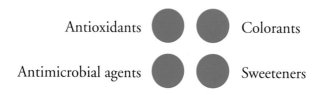

Antioxidants   Colorants

Antimicrobial agents   Sweeteners

Which type of acid serves as the electrolyte in a typical car battery?

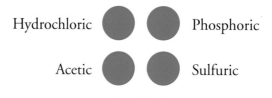

Hydrochloric   Phosphoric

Acetic   Sulfuric

A negatively charged ion is called an anion. What is a positively charged ion called?

Positron   Cation

Electron   Heavion

The Latin name of the brown rat is derived from the name of which European country?

Bulgaria   Denmark

Poland   Norway

English physicist Sir Charles Wheatstone popularized the Wheatstone bridge, a device that accurately measured electrical resistance. He was also the inventor of which musical instrument?

Ukulele   Concertina

Didgeridoo   Xylophone

Which chemist's law states that the amount of a gas absorbed by a liquid is in proportion to the pressure of the gas above the liquid, provided that no chemical action occurs?

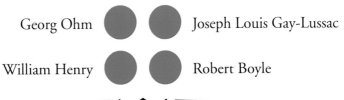

Georg Ohm   Joseph Louis Gay-Lussac

William Henry   Robert Boyle

French singer Yvette Guilbert was the subject of a famous poster showing her in her characteristic yellow dress and long black gloves, painted by which artist?

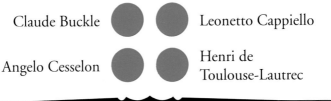

Claude Buckle   Leonetto Cappiello

Angelo Cesselon   Henri de Toulouse-Lautrec

What type of a curve is produced by the intersection of a right circular cone and a plane parallel to an element of the cone?

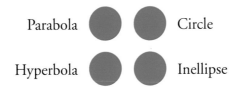

Parabola   Circle

Hyperbola   Inellipse

The Australian silky oak is valued for its flower clusters of what color?

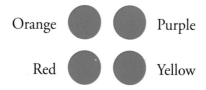

Orange　　　　　　Purple

Red　　　　　　Yellow

In which Italian city would you find the Bargello art museum, especially famous for its collection of Renaissance sculpture?

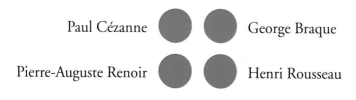

Venice　　　　　　Florence

Rome　　　　　　Milan

Which French painter cofounded the Cubism movement with Spanish artist Pablo Picasso?

Paul Cézanne　　　　　　George Braque

Pierre-Auguste Renoir　　　　　　Henri Rousseau

While many primates have opposable thumbs, which species of monkey is generally thumbless?

Siamang　　　　　　Capuchin

Colobus　　　　　　Marmoset

While Pablo Picasso had his "Blue Period," which other artist decorated the walls of his country house with "black paintings"?

Edouard Manet   Francisco de Goya

Paul Cézanne   Edgar Degas

Which Italian painter, born Alessandro di Mariano Filipepi, used a nickname meaning "little barrel" as his professional name?

Sandro Botticelli   Tintoretto

Andrea del Verrocchio   Antonio Pollaiuolo

Convinced that the secret of the white people's superior power was in written language, Sequoyah devised an alphabet for which Native American language?

Lakota   Cherokee

Navajo   Hopi

Which of these classical composers wrote more than 100 symphonies?

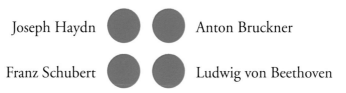

Joseph Haydn   Anton Bruckner

Franz Schubert   Ludwig von Beethoven

Salicin, the source of salicylic acid used in pain relievers, is derived from which tree?

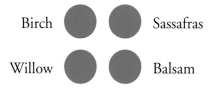

Birch   Sassafras

Willow   Balsam

Nubian, La Mancha, and Toggenburg are breeds of which milk-producing animal?

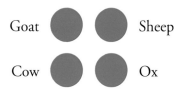

Goat   Sheep

Cow   Ox

What kind of lesson is being taught by Dr. Nicolaes Tulp in a famous 1632 painting by Rembrandt?

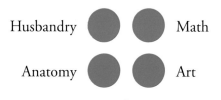

Husbandry   Math

Anatomy   Art

Fado, a traditional musical genre that combines a narrative vocal style with acoustic guitar accompaniment, is native to which country?

Portugal   Sweden

Haiti   Mexico

Japanese-American conductor Seiji Ozawa served as music director for which American orchestra from 1973 to 2002?

American Symphony Orchestra 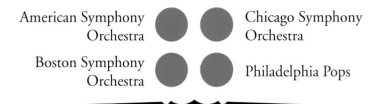 Chicago Symphony Orchestra

Boston Symphony Orchestra

Philadelphia Pops

Which musical direction calls for all voices or a full orchestra?

Da capo 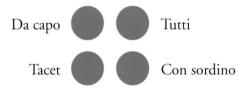 Tutti

Tacet

Con sordino

True tempera is a painting medium incorporating which ingredient?

Egg yolk 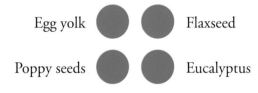 Flaxseed

Poppy seeds

Eucalyptus

Which vitamin is essential for the synthesis of collagen, a protein important in the formation of connective tissue and in wound healing?

A  D

C

E

Which artist's technique for portraying the play of light using tiny brushstrokes of contrasting colors, in works such as *Sunday Afternoon on the Island of La Grande Jatte*, became known as pointillism?

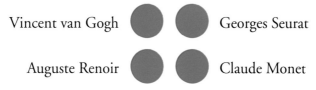

Vincent van Gogh   Georges Seurat

Auguste Renoir   Claude Monet

Which of the five senses is associated with the adjective "gustatory"?

Hearing   Touch

Taste   Sight

What series of unmanned U.S. spacecraft, consisting of 55 scientific satellites launched between 1958 and 1975, included the first artificial satellite launched by the U.S.?

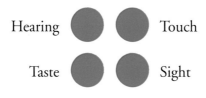

Vanguard   Redstone

Explorer   Voyager

What surname was shared by members of the rock groups Them and the Doors?

Densmore   Manzarek

Krieger   Morrison

What name was shared by the first ship to cross the Atlantic Ocean employing steam power and the first nuclear-powered cargo ship?

Vulcan ⬤ ⬤ United States

Savannah ⬤ ⬤ Cutty Sark

Which U.S. state has 53 mountains higher than 14,000 feet in height, including the famous Pikes Peak?

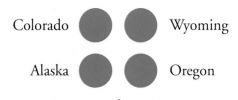

Colorado ⬤ ⬤ Wyoming

Alaska ⬤ ⬤ Oregon

Which of these architecture styles is the oldest?

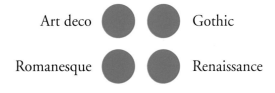

Art deco ⬤ ⬤ Gothic

Romanesque ⬤ ⬤ Renaissance

Who demonstrated, by dropping objects of different weights from the top of the famous Leaning Tower of Pisa, that all falling objects, regardless of size, have the same velocity?

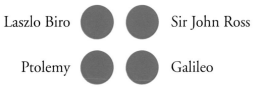

Laszlo Biro ⬤ ⬤ Sir John Ross

Ptolemy ⬤ ⬤ Galileo

Which British explorer and mountaineer, who led early expeditions to Mount Everest, when asked why he wanted to climb the mountain famously replied, "Because it's there"?

Edmund Hillary  Frank Smythe

Robin Hodgkin George Mallory

Who was the lyricist for such classic songs as "I'm an Old Cowhand," "Jeepers Creepers," "That Old Black Magic," and "Moon River"?

Harold Arlen 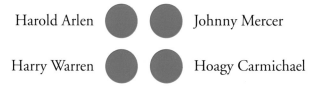 Johnny Mercer

Harry Warren Hoagy Carmichael

The Sigmund Romberg operetta *Blossom Time* was based on the life of which composer and featured songs derived from that composer's works?

Joseph Haydn 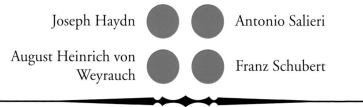 Antonio Salieri

August Heinrich von Weyrauch Franz Schubert

A Roman legion was nominally composed of 6,000 soldiers, and each legion was divided up into 10 what?

Centuria 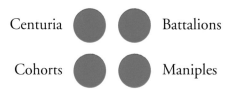 Battalions

Cohorts Maniples

Selman Waksman won the 1952 Nobel Prize for Physiology or Medicine for his codiscovery of what antibiotic that was the first specific agent effective in the treatment of tuberculosis?

Penicillin ● ● Amoxicillin

Cortisporin ● ● Streptomycin

The first name of the English artist who founded the Vorticist movement and the surname used by the author of the science-fiction novel *The Day of the Triffids* are the same. What is the name?

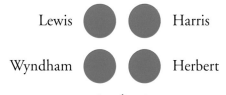

Lewis ● ● Harris

Wyndham ● ● Herbert

In which part of the body would you find the cruciate ligaments?

Knee ● ● Back

Wrist ● ● Ankle

In which year was the last Apollo manned mission to the Moon?

1972 ● ● 1976

1974 ● ● 1978

What singer nicknamed "Empress of the Blues" sold more than 2 million copies of her 1923 hit "Down Hearted Blues"?

Dorothy Dandridge   Bessie Smith

Ma Rainey   Dinah Washington

Which 1950s singer survived the car accident that killed rocker Eddie Cochran in 1960?

Johnnie Ray   Gene Vincent

Jerry Lee Lewis   Cliff Richard

On a computer keyboard, which letter is found furthest right on the lowest row of letter keys?

L   V

M   Z

Which of the following was *not* one of the spaceships flown by Mercury astronauts?

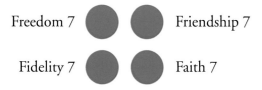

Freedom 7   Friendship 7

Fidelity 7   Faith 7

The eruption of Mount Saint Helens on May 18, 1980, was one of the greatest volcanic explosions ever recorded in North America. In which U.S. state is this volcano located?

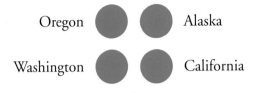

Oregon
Alaska
Washington
California

Nearly three times as wide as Niagara Falls, the spectacular Iguaçu Falls annually attract more than one million foreign and domestic tourists in which country?

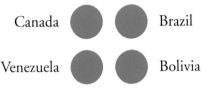

Canada
Brazil
Venezuela
Bolivia

André Derain, Maurice de Vlaminck, and Raoul Dufy were members of which 20th-century art movement identified by the aggressive use of pure, bright colors?

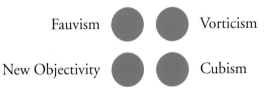

Fauvism
Vorticism
New Objectivity
Cubism

Mammoth Cave, the longest cave system in the world, with more than 345 miles of explored passages, is located in which U.S. state?

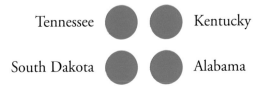

Tennessee
Kentucky
South Dakota
Alabama

An 1891 Leo Tolstoy novella takes its title from which sonata by Beethoven?

Devil's Trill | Appassionata

Feinberg | Kreutzer

Which composer, who bridged the worlds of Classical and Romantic music, wrote the operetta *Die Zwillingsbrüder* (*The Twin Brothers*) and the *Trout Quintet* for piano and strings?

Vincenzo Bellini | Franz Schubert

Felix Mendelssohn | Robert Schumann

The name of which amphibian also refers to a kitchen device for browning food?

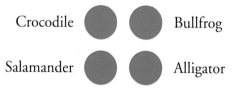

Crocodile | Bullfrog

Salamander | Alligator

A popular distilled liquor known as šljivovica in Europe is made from which fruit?

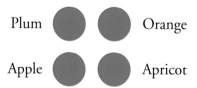

Plum | Orange

Apple | Apricot

Which Dutch artist painted the altarpiece triptych *The Garden of Earthly Delights*, showing earthly paradise with the creation of woman, the first temptation, and the fall of man?

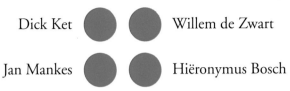

Dick Ket

Willem de Zwart

Jan Mankes

Hiëronymus Bosch

Many of the best-known piano pieces by which German composer were written for his wife, a pianist named Clara?

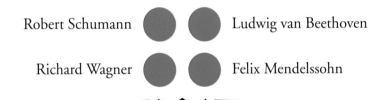

Robert Schumann

Ludwig van Beethoven

Richard Wagner

Felix Mendelssohn

Eustace Tilley, a fictional early American dandy inspired by an illustration in the 11th edition of *Encyclopædia Britannica*, appeared on the cover of the first issue of which popular magazine?

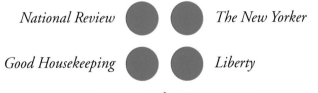

National Review

The New Yorker

Good Housekeeping

Liberty

Who wrote or cowrote the screenplays for the Australian films *Gallipoli* (1981), *Phar Lap* (1982), and *The Year of Living Dangerously* (1982)?

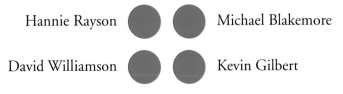

Hannie Rayson

Michael Blakemore

David Williamson

Kevin Gilbert

Which actor starred in the movie *The Truman Show* as a man who discovers that his apparently ordinary life is really a popular reality TV show?

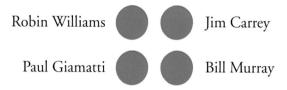

Robin Williams   Jim Carrey

Paul Giamatti   Bill Murray

Which French rococo artist of the 18th century is best known for his works *The Pilgrimage to the Isle of Cythera* and *Gersaint's Shopsign*?

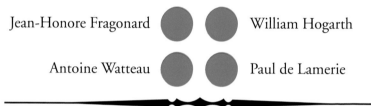

Jean-Honore Fragonard   William Hogarth

Antoine Watteau   Paul de Lamerie

What folk singer was booed off the stage when he tried to play electric guitar at the 1965 Newport Folk Festival?

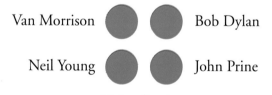

Van Morrison   Bob Dylan

Neil Young   John Prine

How many symphonies were composed by Austrian composer Gustav Mahler?

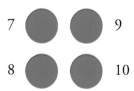

7   9

8   10

Johnny Dodds and Jimmie Noone were jazz musicians noted for playing which instrument?

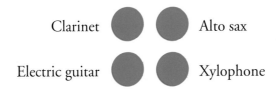

Clarinet   Alto sax

Electric guitar   Xylophone

"Slippery When Wet," "Just to Be Close to You," and "Easy" were three of the seven #1 songs for which soul-funk group?

The Brothers Johnson   Maze

The Average White Band   The Commodores

What actress earned an Academy Award nomination for her debut film performance as a devious Cockney maid in the psychological thriller *Gaslight*?

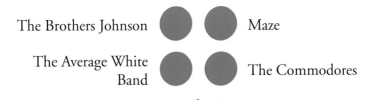

Maggie Smith   Jane Birkin

Angela Lansbury   Glenda Jackson

In March 1914, suffragette Mary Richardson entered the National Gallery in London and attacked which artist's *Rokeby Venus* with a meat cleaver?

Titian   Edouard Manet

Diego Velázquez   Pablo Picasso

What was the surname of British twin brothers Roy and John who produced the films *Brighton Rock*; *Private's Progress*; *I'm All Right, Jack*; and *Seven Days to Noon*?

Tuvey  Harwood

Coen Boulting

The final film released by Britain's Hammer studios was an ill-received remake of which Alfred Hitchcock movie?

The Lodger 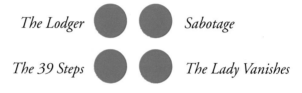 *Sabotage*

The 39 Steps *The Lady Vanishes*

Which composer studied medicine in France, earning a degree in science, before pursuing musical studies, against the wishes of his father, at the Paris Conservatoire?

Alexis de Castillon 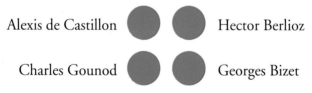 Hector Berlioz

Charles Gounod Georges Bizet

The common ptarmigan is a member of what family of game birds?

Grouse 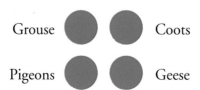 Coots

Pigeons Geese

Lake Baikal is the deepest continental body of water, having a maximum depth of 5,315 feet. In which country is it located?

Ukraine ⬤ ⬤ Russia

Japan ⬤ ⬤ Burma

What duo won the first Grammy Award ever presented in the Rap Performance category?

Run-D.M.C. ⬤ ⬤ DJ Jazzy Jeff and the Fresh Prince

Kris Kross ⬤ ⬤ OutKast

In his first book, *The Selfish Gene*, what zoologist tried to set the record straight on Darwinism, arguing that natural selection did not take place on the level of the species or the individual but rather among genes?

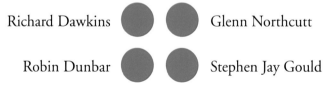

Richard Dawkins ⬤ ⬤ Glenn Northcutt

Robin Dunbar ⬤ ⬤ Stephen Jay Gould

Which of the founding members of Pink Floyd was the first to die, in 2006?

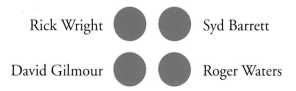

Rick Wright ⬤ ⬤ Syd Barrett

David Gilmour ⬤ ⬤ Roger Waters

What Louisiana native had the top-selling country album of 1994, *Not a Moment Too Soon*, that yielded the hits "Indian Outlaw," "Don't Take the Girl," and "Down on the Farm"?

Randy Travis   Garth Brooks

Tim McGraw   Alan Jackson

Which major moon of Saturn, named after one of the Titans, is noted for its chaotic, tumbling orbit?

Hyperion   Iapetus

Dione   Polydeuces

Composer Antonio Carlos Jobim and guitarist João Gilberto are considered founders of which style of Brazilian popular music that evolved in the late 1950s from a union of samba and cool jazz?

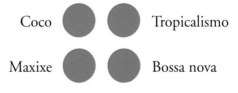

Coco   Tropicalismo

Maxixe   Bossa nova

The mouflon is a wild Mediterranean variety of which animal?

Deer   Pig

Sheep   Antelope

Which artist shows the influence of the Spanish Civil War in works like *The Reaper*, a mural for the Spanish Republic's pavilion at the 1937 Paris World Exhibition, and the nightmarish *Head of a Woman* (1938)?

Joan Miro   Diego Rivera

Pablo Picasso   Paul Klee

Which musical ensemble was made up of Milt Jackson on vibes, John Lewis on piano, Percy Heath on bass, and Connie Kay on drums?

The Four Keys   Modern Jazz Quartet

The Dave Brubeck Quartet   The Deardorf Peterson Group

What musician, born James Osterberg, was the leader of the punk rock group the Stooges?

Iggy Pop   Lou Reed

David Bowie   Rod Stewart

What suave performer costarred with Jeanette MacDonald in the early movie musicals *The Love Parade*, *One Hour With You*, *Love Me Tonight*, and *The Merry Widow*?

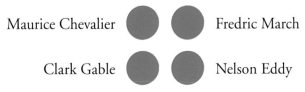

Maurice Chevalier   Fredric March

Clark Gable   Nelson Eddy

Jean Arthur played cynical newspaper reporter Babe Bennett who writes mocking stories about a shy man who inherits millions of dollars, but ends up falling in love with the man in what 1936 movie?

Meet John Doe

Mr. Smith Goes to Washington

Mr. Deeds Goes to Town

The Man Who Came to Dinner

Which brand of ale is featured in the 1960 sculpture *Painted Bronze* and the 1964 painting *Ale Cans* by artist Jasper Johns?

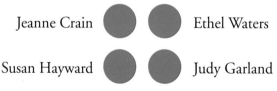

Labatt's

Moosehead

Molson Golden

Ballantine

Which actress earned a Best Actress Academy Award nomination for her starring role as a young black woman passing for white in the controversial 1949 film *Pinky*?

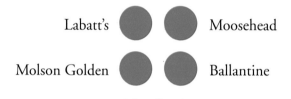

Jeanne Crain

Ethel Waters

Susan Hayward

Judy Garland

Encyclopædia Britannica divides the life of which composer into the Arnstadt period, Mühlhausen period, Weimar period, and Köthen period?

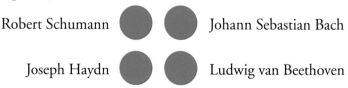

Robert Schumann

Johann Sebastian Bach

Joseph Haydn

Ludwig van Beethoven

Which term is used to describe a misshapen pearl or a 17th-century period of the arts?

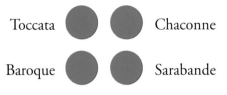

Toccata   Chaconne

Baroque   Sarabande

What leading composer from Finland wrote the 1899 tone poem *Finlandia*?

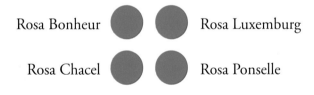

Granville Bantock   Karl Goldmark

Robert Fuchs   Jean Sibelius

Which of these women named Rosa was a noted coloratura soprano?

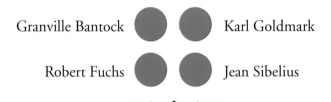

Rosa Bonheur   Rosa Luxemburg

Rosa Chacel   Rosa Ponselle

Which TV orchestra leader founded and conducted the New York Pops?

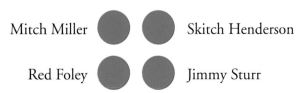

Mitch Miller   Skitch Henderson

Red Foley   Jimmy Sturr

Levi Stubbs was the lead vocalist for which Motown group?

The Miracles 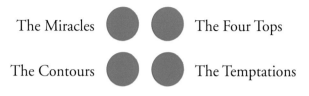 The Four Tops

The Contours The Temptations

"Sit Down, You're Rockin' the Boat" and "Adelaide's Lament" are songs from which Broadway musical?

The Pajama Game 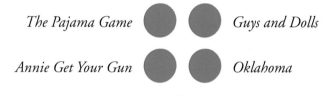 *Guys and Dolls*

Annie Get Your Gun *Oklahoma*

Which of the following is *not* a type of bird?

Lory  Tody

Cony Coly

Which instrument was played by cool jazz musician Gerry Mulligan?

French horn  Piano

Tuba Baritone sax

Which actress won an Academy Award for Best Actress for her film debut in 1931, and won an Academy Award for Best Supporting Actress in 1970?

Fay Wray · Helen Hayes

Gloria Stuart · Sylvia Sidney

Blues performer Sonny Boy Williamson was a self-taught virtuoso on which musical instrument?

Guitar · Piano

Harmonica · Banjo

Which film comedy starred Bette Midler, Diane Keaton, and Goldie Hawn as former college friends bent on revenge against their ex-husbands?

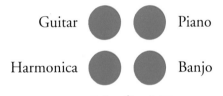

The Lemon Sisters · *Ruthless People*

Outrageous Fortune · *The First Wives Club*

Which feminist artist's best-known piece is *The Dinner Party*, presenting a large triangular table placed on 999 ceramic plates with place settings for 39 notable women?

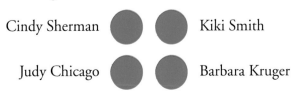

Cindy Sherman · Kiki Smith

Judy Chicago · Barbara Kruger

"Anarchy in the U.K.," "Pretty Vacant," and "Holidays in the Sun" were singles from which British rock group?

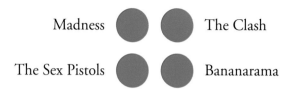

Madness   The Clash

The Sex Pistols   Bananarama

Who was the lead singer for the Sugarcubes, whose acclaimed first album, *Life's Too Good*, was released in 1986?

Pink   Enya

Björk   Frida

Popular as a cooked vegetable in Europe, the Jerusalem artichoke is an edible tuber of which plant?

Sunflower   Mustard

Taro   Rose

Which participant in atomic bomb research at the Manhattan Project was awarded a Nobel Prize in Physics for his work with quantum electrodynamics?

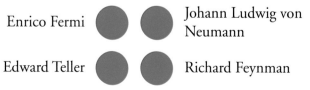

Enrico Fermi   Johann Ludwig von Neumann

Edward Teller   Richard Feynman

Which substance acts as a catalyst for chemical reactions in living organisms?

Enzyme   Lipid

Vitamin   Nucleobase

In which movie did actor Laurence Olivier and director Alfred Hitchcock work together?

The Lodger   *Jamaica Inn*

Blackmail   *Rebecca*

Which rap group's self-titled debut album was the first rap album to attain gold status with sales of more than 500,000 copies?

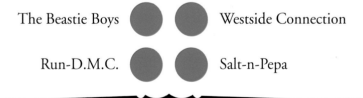

The Beastie Boys   Westside Connection

Run-D.M.C.   Salt-n-Pepa

The Burgess Shale is one of the best preserved fossil formations in the world, with more than 60,000 specimens retrieved from the bed since 1909. In which country is it located?

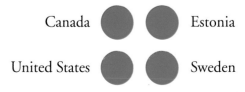

Canada   Estonia

United States   Sweden

"Summertime," "It Ain't Necessarily So," and "I Got Plenty o' Nuttin'" are song standards originally featured in which George Gershwin musical?

Girl Crazy   *Strike Up the Band*

Porgy and Bess   *Of Thee I Sing*

In classical architecture, which term refers to a draped female figure used instead of a column as a support?

Caryatid   Telamon

Obelisk   Plinth

Which author's *The Moon and Sixpence* was suggested by the life of artist Paul Gauguin?

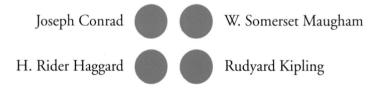

Joseph Conrad   W. Somerset Maugham

H. Rider Haggard   Rudyard Kipling

Which cloud of gas in space is the remnants of a supernova occurring in A.D. 1054, seen in one of the horns of the constellation Taurus?

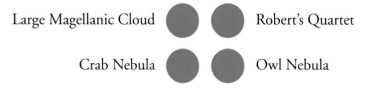

Large Magellanic Cloud   Robert's Quartet

Crab Nebula   Owl Nebula

Mount Erebus is the most active volcano on which continent?

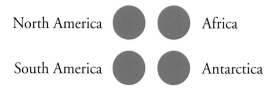

North America   Africa

South America   Antarctica

Prior to his work with the Morse Code, Samuel F.B. Morse was an art professor at the University of the City of New York. Morse worked primarily with which form of art?

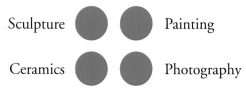

Sculpture   Painting

Ceramics   Photography

The Andy Warhol Museum opened in 1994 in which city believed to be Warhol's hometown?

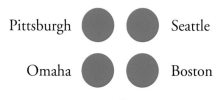

Pittsburgh   Seattle

Omaha   Boston

Which composer's seventh symphony, *Sinfonia Antarctica* (1953), was an adaptation of his music for the film *Scott of the Antarctic*?

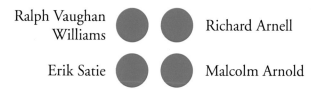

Ralph Vaughan Williams   Richard Arnell

Erik Satie   Malcolm Arnold

After his mother's death, what Russian composer shared a small flat with Nikolay Rimsky-Korsakov until 1872, whereupon he sank into an alcoholic depression when his colleague married and moved out?

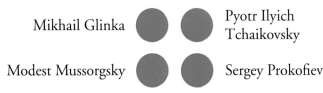

Mikhail Glinka   Pyotr Ilyich Tchaikovsky

Modest Mussorgsky   Sergey Prokofiev

Which pop singer's self-titled debut album featured three #1 songs: "Greatest Love of All," "Saving All My Love for You," and "How Will I Know"?

Madonna   Whitney Houston

Christina Aguilera   Mariah Carey

Which actor played Bette Davis's psychiatrist in *Now, Voyager* and played her loving husband in *Mr. Skeffington*?

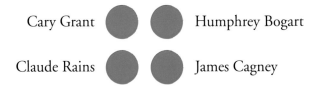

Cary Grant   Humphrey Bogart

Claude Rains   James Cagney

Which classical musician wrote his autobiography, *My First 79 Years*, in 1999, with the aid of novelist Chaim Potok?

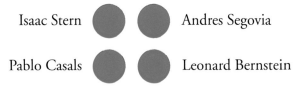

Isaac Stern   Andres Segovia

Pablo Casals   Leonard Bernstein

Missionary Albert Schweitzer was an accomplished musician on which instrument, having studied under Charles-Marie Widor?

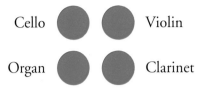

Cello　　　Violin

Organ　　　Clarinet

Which of the Muppets worked as a street reporter on *Sesame Street* and served as the host of *The Muppet Show*?

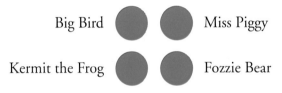

Big Bird　　　Miss Piggy

Kermit the Frog　　　Fozzie Bear

Which ballerina married Roberto Emilio Arias, former Panamanian ambassador to Great Britain in 1955, and died 36 years later in Panama City?

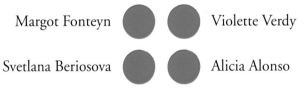

Margot Fonteyn　　　Violette Verdy

Svetlana Beriosova　　　Alicia Alonso

Which supermodel was the second wife of singer Billy Joel, and made an appearance in his music video for "Uptown Girl"?

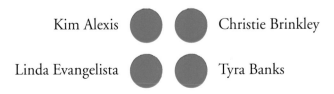

Kim Alexis　　　Christie Brinkley

Linda Evangelista　　　Tyra Banks

Which composer managed with great difficulty to finish the last of his oratorios, *Jephtha*, in 1752 as he battled with failing eyesight?

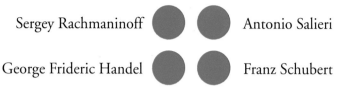

Sergey Rachmaninoff   Antonio Salieri

George Frideric Handel   Franz Schubert

Janet Jackson sampled from which Joni Mitchell song for her hit song "Got 'Til It's Gone"?

"Big Yellow Taxi"   "Dog Eat Dog"

"Woodstock"   "Both Sides Now"

In astronomy, which constellation falls between Cancer and Virgo?

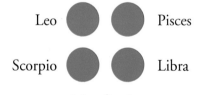

Leo   Pisces

Scorpio   Libra

Which actor exhibited his skill in fencing in the movies *The Three Musketeers* (1921), *Don Q, Son of Zorro* (1925), *The Black Pirate* (1926), and *The Iron Mask* (1929)?

Ramon Novarro   John Gilbert

Rudolph Valentino   Douglas Fairbanks Sr.

Posdnuos, Trugoy the Dove, and Pasemaster Mase are members of what influential hip-hop group formed in Amityville, New York, in 1988?

The Beastie Boys   De La Soul

Public Enemy   A Tribe Called Quest

Irving Stone's *Lust for Life* was a fictionalized biography of which painter?

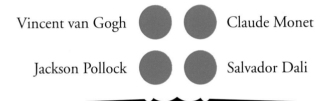

Vincent van Gogh   Claude Monet

Jackson Pollock   Salvador Dali

Which musical instrument was played by Efrem Zimbalist Sr. and Jascha Heifetz?

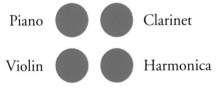

Piano   Clarinet

Violin   Harmonica

Which singer's final hit, "Garden Party" in 1972, described his frustration with the hostile reaction of the audience at an "oldies" concert?

Rick Nelson   Neil Sedaka

Sam Cooke   John Lennon

Former rock journalist Chrissie Hynde made her mark as the lead singer for which new wave rock group?

The Go-Go's ⬤ ⬤ The Pretenders

Heaven 17 ⬤ ⬤ Blondie

Actress Maureen O'Sullivan, best remembered for her film portrayal of Jane opposite Johnny Weissmuller in his title role as Tarzan, is the mother of which actress?

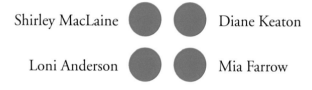

Shirley MacLaine ⬤ ⬤ Diane Keaton

Loni Anderson ⬤ ⬤ Mia Farrow

Which actor won an Academy Award for playing the title role of the charlatan evangelist Elmer Gantry?

Jack Lemmon ⬤ ⬤ Burt Lancaster

Trevor Howard ⬤ ⬤ Spencer Tracy

Conway Twitty produced a string of duets with which female singer, notably "Louisiana Woman, Mississippi Man" and "After the Fire Is Gone," the latter of which won them a 1971 Grammy Award?

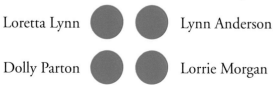

Loretta Lynn ⬤ ⬤ Lynn Anderson

Dolly Parton ⬤ ⬤ Lorrie Morgan

The practices of shiatsu and acupuncture are intended to improve the flow of the body energy, or chi, through how many pathways in the human body?

3

9

6

12

Which Hollywood musical star played dramatic roles in the movies *On the Beach* (1959), *The Pleasure of His Company* (1962), and *The Towering Inferno* (1974)?

Judy Garland

Fred Astaire

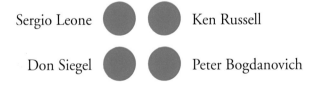

Gene Kelly

Janet Gaynor

Clint Eastwood worked with which director on the movies *Coogan's Bluff*, *Two Mules for Sister Sara*, *The Beguiled*, and *Escape From Alcatraz*?

Sergio Leone

Ken Russell

Don Siegel

Peter Bogdanovich

After jazz drummer Chick Webb died in 1939, who took over leadership of his band until it broke up in 1942?

Duke Ellington

Ella Fitzgerald

Mel Tormé

Dizzy Gillespie

Which psychedelic rock band recorded the 1967 hit singles "Somebody to Love" and "White Rabbit"?

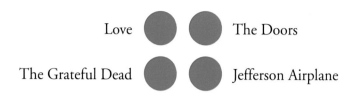

Love

The Doors

The Grateful Dead

Jefferson Airplane

Who played the title roles in the 1960s film comedies *The Bellboy*, *The Errand Boy*, and *The Nutty Professor*?

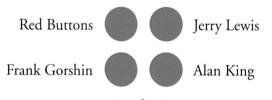

Red Buttons

Jerry Lewis

Frank Gorshin

Alan King

"A Whole New World" won the 1992 Oscar for Best Original Song for which animated Disney film?

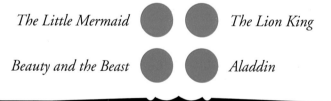

The Little Mermaid

The Lion King

Beauty and the Beast

Aladdin

Which singer's 1971 album *Every Picture Tells a Story* became the first record to top the charts in Britain and the United States simultaneously?

Rod Stewart

Glen Campbell

Jim Croce

Elton John

Which singer won record of the year and song of the year Grammy Awards in 1998 for "Sunny Came Home"?

Natasha Bedingfield 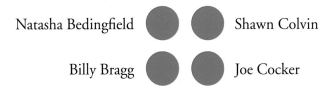 Shawn Colvin

Billy Bragg Joe Cocker

Who was the only director to win two Best Director Oscars during the 1980s?

Woody Allen 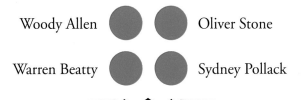 Oliver Stone

Warren Beatty Sydney Pollack

What movie costarred sex symbol Marilyn Monroe and thespian Laurence Olivier?

How to Marry a Millionaire 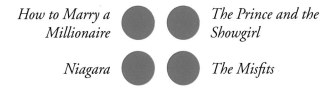 *The Prince and the Showgirl*

Niagara *The Misfits*

What was the first full-length animated film released by Walt Disney and company?

Bambi  *Fantasia*

Pinocchio *Snow White and the Seven Dwarfs*

Which actress won a Tony Award in 1954 for playing a water nymph opposite husband Mel Ferrer in *Ondine*, her final Broadway play?

Mary Martin 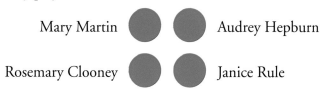 Audrey Hepburn

Rosemary Clooney Janice Rule

What singer of "Pata Pata" was married to trumpeter Hugh Masekela and black activist Stokely Carmichael?

Billie Holiday 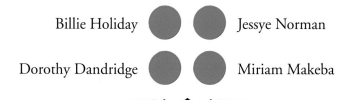 Jessye Norman

Dorothy Dandridge Miriam Makeba

"With or Without You" and "I Still Haven't Found What I'm Looking For" were #1 songs off of which U2 album?

Achtung Baby 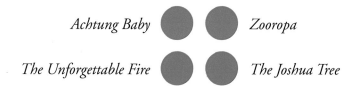 *Zooropa*

The Unforgettable Fire *The Joshua Tree*

Whose works of photography are collected in *Observations* (1959), with a text by Truman Capote, and in *Nothing Personal* (1976), with a text by James Baldwin?

Robert Mapplethorpe 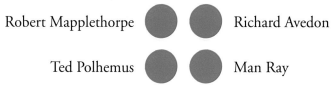 Richard Avedon

Ted Polhemus Man Ray

Who directed film adaptations of the Paddy Chayefsky teleplays *Marty* and *The Bachelor Party*, winning an Oscar for Best Director with the former?

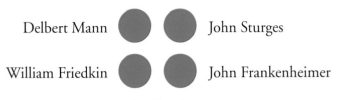

Delbert Mann   John Sturges

William Friedkin   John Frankenheimer

Which pop singer reputedly wrote his hit song "Splish Splash" in only 12 minutes?

Jerry Wallace   Tommy Edwards

Bobby Darin   Neil Sedaka

Actor James MacArthur, who played the cop nicknamed Danno on *Hawaii Five-O*, is the son of which actress?

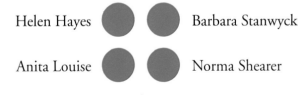

Helen Hayes   Barbara Stanwyck

Anita Louise   Norma Shearer

Which veteran movie director was behind the helm for the science-fiction films *The Day the Earth Stood Still* in 1951, *The Andromeda Strain* in 1971, and the first *Star Trek* movie in 1979?

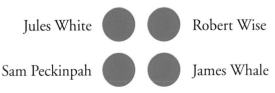

Jules White   Robert Wise

Sam Peckinpah   James Whale

In the 1950s, which actress played a scheming actress in *All About Eve* and a scheming princess in *The Ten Commandments*?

Janet Leigh   Judith Anderson

Debra Paget   Anne Baxter

Which actor played the other half of a song-and-dance team with Bing Crosby in the holiday film *White Christmas*?

Danny Kaye   Gene Kelly

Bob Hope   Dick Van Dyke

Who rewrote his short play *Still Life* as the 1946 film *Brief Encounter*?

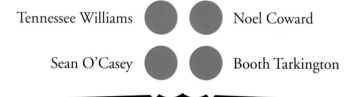

Tennessee Williams   Noel Coward

Sean O'Casey   Booth Tarkington

In 1994, the Metropolitan Opera stunned many opera fans with the terse announcement that it had fired which soprano for what it termed "unprofessional actions"?

Joan Sutherland   Adelina Patti

Kathleen Battle   Loulie Jean Norman

Which *American Idol* alum sang the National Anthem at the 2008 Democratic Convention and the 2009 Super Bowl?

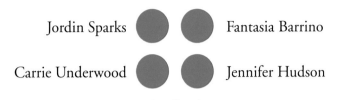

Jordin Sparks   Fantasia Barrino

Carrie Underwood   Jennifer Hudson

Mark Knopfler was the vocalist and lead guitarist for which rock band?

Kings of Leon   Dire Straits

Oasis   Simple Minds

"Mood Indigo," "Black and Tan Fantasy," "Creole Love Call," and "Rockin' in Rhythm" were among the classic songs performed by which bandleader during his years at the Cotton Club in Harlem?

Cab Calloway   Duke Ellington

Count Basie   Louis Armstrong

Who sang the theme songs for three different James Bond movies?

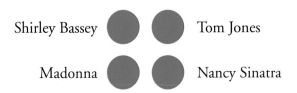

Shirley Bassey   Tom Jones

Madonna   Nancy Sinatra

What was the only movie produced and directed by Cecil B. DeMille to win an Oscar for Best Picture?

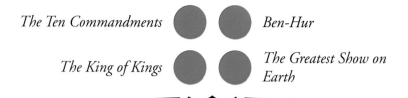

The Ten Commandments ⬤ ⬤ *Ben-Hur*

The King of Kings ⬤ ⬤ *The Greatest Show on Earth*

Which actress's love affair with the Italian director Roberto Rossellini, during the filming of *Stromboli* in 1950, led to a scandal that forced her to move to Europe?

Greta Garbo ⬤ ⬤ Ingrid Bergman

Sophia Loren ⬤ ⬤ Marlene Dietrich

Who was the band leader for the Royal Canadians, playing "the sweetest music this side of heaven"?

Ray Noble ⬤ ⬤ Tommy Dorsey

Kid Ory ⬤ ⬤ Guy Lombardo

Which of these jazz musicians was *not* noted for playing the saxophone?

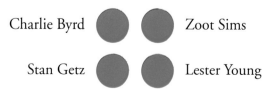

Charlie Byrd ⬤ ⬤ Zoot Sims

Stan Getz ⬤ ⬤ Lester Young

Which band leader commissioned George Gershwin's *Rhapsody in Blue* and conducted its premiere at Aeolian Hall, New York City, in 1924, with the composer as piano soloist?

Louis Armstrong   Paul Whiteman

Glenn Miller   Benny Goodman

Which actor earned his big break in 1994 when he was cast as Dr. Doug Ross on the TV drama *ER*?

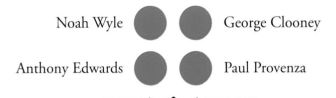

Noah Wyle   George Clooney

Anthony Edwards   Paul Provenza

Which TV game show host claimed to have been a hit man for the CIA?

Pat Sajak   Chuck Barris

Howie Mandel   Richard Dawson

Angel Falls, the highest waterfall in the world, is situated in Venezuela. In which country is Tugela Falls, the second highest waterfall in the world, located?

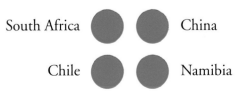

South Africa   China

Chile   Namibia

In 1990, José Carreras, Luciano Pavarotti, and Placido Domingo first performed together billed as the "Three Tenors." The concert was held at the World Cup football championship in which city?

Madrid   Montevideo

Mexico City   Rome

Which actor accepted his Academy Award saying "I would like to be Jupiter and kidnap everybody and lie down in the firmament making love to everybody"?

Tom Hanks   Roberto Benigni

Peter Sellers   Jack Palance

What title is shared by a Rainer Werner Fassbinder film of the 1980s and a hit song for the Kinks in the 1970s?

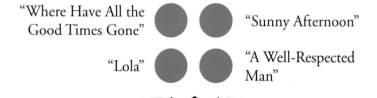

"Where Have All the Good Times Gone"   "Sunny Afternoon"

"Lola"   "A Well-Respected Man"

Calvados is a brandy made from which fruit?

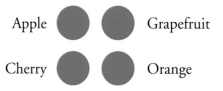

Apple   Grapefruit

Cherry   Orange

Which country singer's album *Drive* included the song "Drive (for Daddy Gene)," which paid tribute to his father, a mechanic who worked in a Ford plant?

Vince Gill   Charley Pride

Randy Travis   Alan Jackson

Which actor appeared with Russell Crowe and Al Pacino, playing TV journalist Mike Wallace, in the 1999 movie *The Insider*?

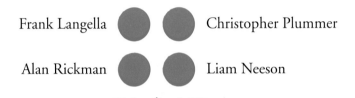

Frank Langella   Christopher Plummer

Alan Rickman   Liam Neeson

Which R&B singer had hits in the 1960s with "Cry Cry Cry," "I Pity the Fool," "Turn On Your Love Light," and "That's the Way Love Is" for Duke Records?

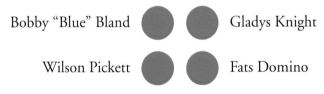

Bobby "Blue" Bland   Gladys Knight

Wilson Pickett   Fats Domino

Which 2008 movie reunited Kate Winslet with her *Titanic* costar Leonardo DiCaprio?

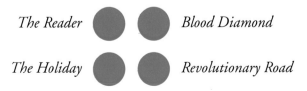

The Reader   *Blood Diamond*

The Holiday   *Revolutionary Road*

Pierce Brosnan, who portrayed James Bond in three movies, was married to Cassandra Harris, an actress who had a role in which earlier James Bond movie?

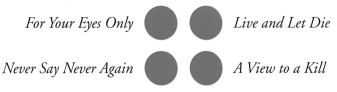

For Your Eyes Only

Live and Let Die

Never Say Never Again

A View to a Kill

Which author famously described his introduction to psychedelic drugs in his book *The Doors of Perception*?

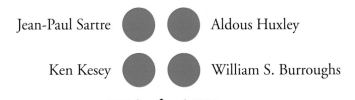

Jean-Paul Sartre

Aldous Huxley

Ken Kesey

William S. Burroughs

Which girl group from New Orleans had a hit in 1964 with "Chapel of Love"?

The Shangri-Las

The Dixie Cups

The Marvelettes

The Crystals

Which actress worked with her mother in the horror films *The Fog* (1980) and *Halloween H20: 20 Years Later* (1998)?

Angelina Jolie

Adrienne Barbeau

Jamie Lee Curtis

Trish Van Devere

Which Woody Allen movie was a parody of 19th-century Russian novels?

Love and Death   Stardust Memories

September   Zelig

Which actress was married to Alfred Steele, the chairman of the Pepsi-Cola Company, and after his death in 1959, became a director of the company?

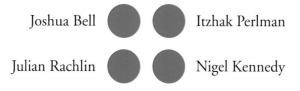

Bette Davis   Joan Crawford

Jane Wyman   Rosalind Russell

Which violin virtuoso played the solo violin passages in John Williams's Oscar-winning score for the movie *Schindler's List*?

Joshua Bell   Itzhak Perlman

Julian Rachlin   Nigel Kennedy

Which film director developed a cult following with his three low-budget horror films *Bad Taste* (1987), *Meet the Feebles* (1989), and *Braindead* (1992)?

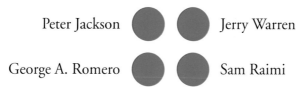

Peter Jackson   Jerry Warren

George A. Romero   Sam Raimi

Prior to her solo debut with *The Miseducation of Lauryn Hill*, singer Lauryn Hill was a member of which hip-hop soul group?

The Black Eyed Peas 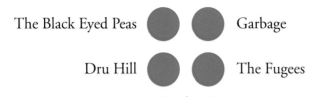 Garbage

Dru Hill The Fugees

Which actor, who originated the role of the domineering Big Daddy on Broadway in *Cat on a Hot Tin Roof*, reprised his powerful performance for the 1958 film version?

Melvyn Douglas  Burl Ives

Paul Newman George C. Scott

What jazz singer, selected by Miles Davis as his opening act in the 1960s, won a 1998 Grammy Award for her album *I Remember Miles*?

Sarah Vaughan  Nina Simone

Shirley Horn June Christy

Known primarily as an author of tragic plays, Jean Racine wrote which three-act comedy in 1668?

Bajazet 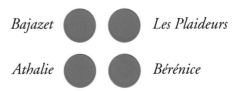 *Les Plaideurs*

Athalie *Bérénice*

Which playwright's collaboration with George S. Kaufman produced such popular comedies as *You Can't Take It With You* and *The Man Who Came to Dinner*?

Charles MacArthur 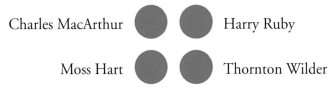 Harry Ruby

Moss Hart Thornton Wilder

Which singer wrote books about working with Judy Garland and Buddy Rich, and published his autobiography, *It Wasn't All Velvet*, in 1988?

Ray Bolger 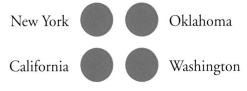 Nat King Cole

Mel Tormé Jack Haley Jr.

The Woodstock Music Festival entertained about 400,000 young rock fans and was a high point of the American youth counterculture of the 1960s. In which U.S. state did this concert event take place?

New York  Oklahoma

California Washington

Which actress was the first black woman to win a Tony Award for Best Actress, for her role as matriarch Lena Younger in Lorraine Hansberry's *A Raisin in the Sun*?

Phylicia Rashad 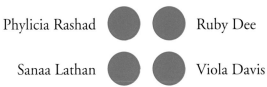 Ruby Dee

Sanaa Lathan Viola Davis

The hype over the release of his 1975 album *Born to Run* landed which singer on the covers of the magazines *Time* and *Newsweek* in the same week?

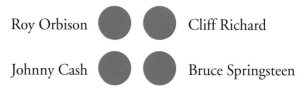

Roy Orbison   Cliff Richard

Johnny Cash   Bruce Springsteen

Which actor displayed his versatility by playing a homosexual hooligan in *My Beautiful Laundrette* and a staid Edwardian-era Englishman in *A Room With a View* in the same year?

Mel Gibson   Daniel Day-Lewis

Jude Law   Jeremy Irons

In what 2002 movie did Nicolas Cage play twin brothers?

Next   *Face/Off*

Windtalkers   *Adaptation*

Which country singer has sold more than 7 million copies of her album *Breathe*, which debuted at the #1 spot on the Billboard country album chart and on the Billboard 200 charts in 1999?

LeAnn Rimes   Faith Hill

Chely Wright   Emmylou Harris

The chief commercial method of producing which material is by the Haber-Bosch process, which involves the direct reaction of elemental hydrogen and elemental nitrogen?

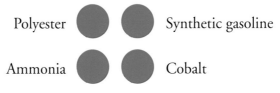

Polyester　　　　　　Synthetic gasoline

Ammonia　　　　　　Cobalt

On *The Simpsons*, which musical instrument does Lisa Simpson play?

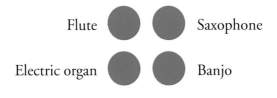

Flute　　　　　　Saxophone

Electric organ　　　　　　Banjo

What patriotic cartoonist was 16 years old when he was sent to France by the Red Cross to drive an ambulance during World War I?

Charles Schulz　　　　　　Milton Caniff

Walt Disney　　　　　　Al Capp

Modern mariners' compasses are usually mounted in what pedestals that contain specially placed magnets and pieces of steel that cancel the magnetic effects of the metal of the ship?

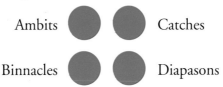

Ambits　　　　　　Catches

Binnacles　　　　　　Diapasons

Which Apollo flight was the first to make a lunar orbit?

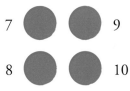

7   8   9   10

Ciguatera is a form of food poisoning associated with the eating of which item?

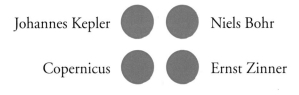

Pork   Dairy products

Tomatoes   Fish

Which German astronomer discovered three major laws of planetary motion?

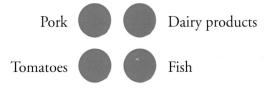

Johannes Kepler   Niels Bohr

Copernicus   Ernst Zinner

Scurvy, one of the oldest-known nutritional disorders of humankind, is caused by a dietary lack of which vitamin?

C   E

D   K

On the periodic table, which element is directly below copper and directly above gold?

Cobalt   Nickel

Silver   Iron

Edmund Gunter, William Oughtred, and Robert Bissaker devised some of the earlier versions of which tool?

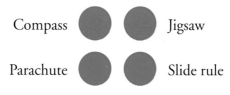

Compass   Jigsaw

Parachute   Slide rule

What liquid is issued from the lachrymal glands?

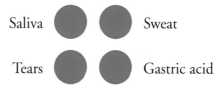

Saliva   Sweat

Tears   Gastric acid

Whose law of physics states that pressure applied to a confined liquid is transmitted undiminished through the liquid in all directions regardless of the area to which the pressure is applied?

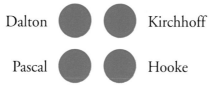

Dalton   Kirchhoff

Pascal   Hooke

Which farm animals may be descendants of the extinct auroch?

Sheep   Chickens

Cattle   Pigs

William Harvey's greatest medical achievement was the discovery of which system within the human body?

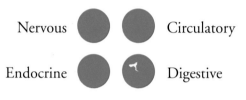

Nervous   Circulatory

Endocrine   Digestive

The magnetic South Pole is not stationary, but rather moves about how many miles to the northwest each year?

8   30

17   69

What kind of pendulum is suspended from a long line mounted so that its perpendicular plane of swing rotates in relation to the Earth's surface?

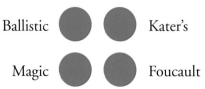

Ballistic   Kater's

Magic   Foucault

The Babinski response is the only abnormal reflex that is routinely detected by physicians. On which part of the body is this reflex tested?

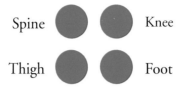

Spine   Knee

Thigh   Foot

Quinine, a drug obtained from cinchona bark, is used chiefly in the treatment of which disease?

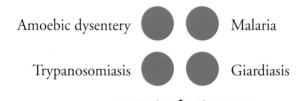

Amoebic dysentery   Malaria

Trypanosomiasis   Giardiasis

Which flightless bird was exterminated from the island of Mauritius, and rendered extinct, in 1681?

Moa   Kagu

Elephant bird   Dodo

What is the name of the hypothetical boundary dividing the zoogeographical regions of Asia and Australasia?

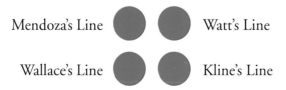

Mendoza's Line   Watt's Line

Wallace's Line   Kline's Line

Composed of fatty materials, protein, and water, what is the white, insulating sheath on the axon of many neurons?

Myelin   Fimbria

Glair   Pallium

Which of these French composers was *not* a member of the group known as *Les Six*?

Francis Poulenc   Darius Milhaud

Erik Satie   Arthur Honegger

Which artist, deeply influenced by modern industrial technology and Cubism, developed "machine art," a style characterized by monumental mechanistic forms rendered in bold colors?

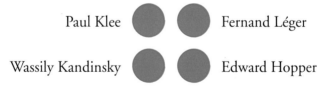

Paul Klee   Fernand Léger

Wassily Kandinsky   Edward Hopper

The central component in what device consists of an evacuated glass container with phosphorescent coating at one end and an electron gun and a system for focusing and deflecting the electron beam at the other?

Oscilloscope   Thermostat

Geiger counter   Galvanometer

In Zen Buddhism of Japan, what name is given to a succinct paradoxical statement or question used as a meditation discipline for novices, such as "What is the sound of one hand clapping?"

Dogen   Bokuseki

Koan   Sensei

Beethoven's 9th and final symphony, incorporating his *Ode to Joy*, was written in which key?

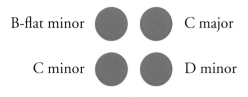

B-flat minor   C major

C minor   D minor

Which island is noted for its large collection of standing moai statues?

Jemo Island   Easter Island

Wallis Island   Iwo Jima

The Nazca Lines, a group of large line drawings and geometric figures visible only from the air, are etched into the Earth's surface in which country?

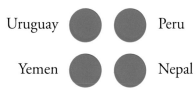

Uruguay   Peru

Yemen   Nepal

What was the surname of the lead singer in the Motown group Martha and the Vandellas?

Robinson 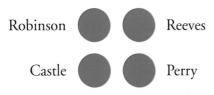 Reeves

Castle Perry

Which nuclear particle consists of two down quarks and one up quark?

Electron  Proton

Neutron Pi meson

What kind of computer software translates source code written in a high-level language (e.g., C++) into a set of machine-language instructions that can be understood by a digital computer's CPU?

Binder 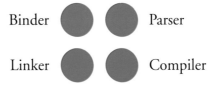 Parser

Linker Compiler

Which kind of acid occurs in the blood when glycogen is broken down in muscle and can be converted back to glycogen in the liver?

Acetic  Boric

Lactic Amino

What term is used in architecture to describe ornamentation in scroll form and also refers to an oval frame enclosing the hieroglyphs of the name of an Egyptian sovereign?

Medallion   Spandrel

Guilloché   Cartouche

In physics, what is equal to the mass of an object multiplied by its velocity and is equivalent to the force required to bring the object to a stop in a unit length of time?

Flux   Turbidity

Momentum   Density

Newton's first law says a body at rest or moving at a constant speed in a straight line will remain at rest or keep moving in a straight line at constant speed unless acted on by a force. This is called the law of what?

Inertia   Relativity

Dynamics   Astrophysics

The carving of kachina dolls and the performance of the snake dance are associated with which Indian tribe?

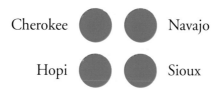

Cherokee   Navajo

Hopi   Sioux

Johann Blumenbach, often called the father of physical anthropology, proposed one of the earliest classifications of mankind. Through the study of skulls, he divided mankind into how many families?

3 6

5 7

Parchment was originally created by processing animal skins as writing material. Parchment made from the more delicate skins of calf or kid came to be called what?

Klaf Gevil

Vellum Papyrus

Which moon of Neptune is similar in size, density, and surface composition to the dwarf planet Pluto, and is thought to have been formed elsewhere in the solar system and later captured by Neptune?

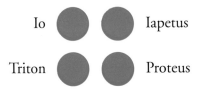

Io Iapetus

Triton Proteus

Among the most common phobias are acrophobia, fear of high places; claustrophobia, fear of closed places; and ochlophobia, fear of what?

Spiders Crowds

Clowns Mice

During the 1860s and '70s what painter began to use musical terms in titling works like *Nocturne in Black and Gold: The Falling Rocket* and his most famous, *Arrangement in Grey and Black, No. 1: The Artist's Mother?*

James McNeill Whistler   John Singer Sargent

Winslow Homer   William Merritt Chase

Which jazz performer's best-known composition was his theme song, "Artistry in Rhythm"?

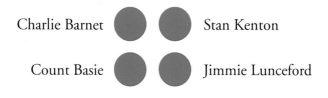

Charlie Barnet   Stan Kenton

Count Basie   Jimmie Lunceford

The double-ringed Vivaldi crater and the 960-mile-wide Caloris basin are features on the surface of which planet?

Mercury   Mars

Venus   Neptune

Who wrote the country music standards "Hello Walls," "Night Life," "Funny How Time Slips Away," and "Crazy"?

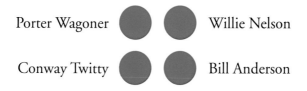

Porter Wagoner   Willie Nelson

Conway Twitty   Bill Anderson

Which country singer wrote "Okie From Muskogee," his best-known recording, a novelty song that became controversial for its apparent attack on hippies?

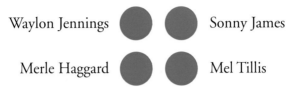

Waylon Jennings   Sonny James

Merle Haggard   Mel Tillis

Pelléas et Mélisande, first performed in 1902, was the only opera written by which composer?

Claude Debussy   Maurice Ravel

Georges Bizet   Francis Poulenc

What is a male giraffe called?

Rig   Rat

Stud   Bull

Which composer is best known for his three ballets based on American folk material: *Billy the Kid* (1938), *Rodeo* (1942), and *Appalachian Spring* (1944)?

Aaron Copland   Woody Herman

Van Cliburn   Leonard Bernstein

Which of these mammals usually gives birth to twins, rather than a single offspring?

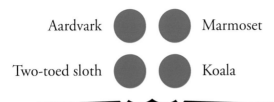

Aardvark　　　Marmoset

Two-toed sloth　　　Koala

What arthritis drug was removed from the market in 2004 after the discovery that people who took the drug for more than 18 months had twice the risk of heart attack and stroke than those who took a placebo?

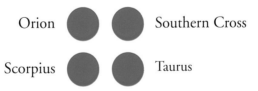

Fen-Phen　　　Vioxx

Crestor　　　Accutane

Several hundred times larger than the Sun, Antares is the brightest star in which constellation?

Orion　　　Southern Cross

Scorpius　　　Taurus

In physics, what is the change in direction of a wave passing from one medium to another caused by its change in speed?

Fission　　　Torque

Refraction　　　Reflection

Civil engineer Washington Augustus Roebling finished construction in 1883 on which bridge that was designed by his father, John Augustus Roebling?

Mackinac Bridge 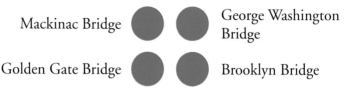 George Washington Bridge

Golden Gate Bridge Brooklyn Bridge

The Great Barrier Reef runs along which shore of the Australian continent?

Northeast  Southeast

Northwest Southwest

In plants, which layer of tissue lies between the surface cells and the vascular, or conducting, tissues of stems and roots?

Xylem  Cortex

Phloem Pith

In 1967 the World Health Organization began a global vaccination program against which disease and declared it officially eradicated in 1980?

Malaria 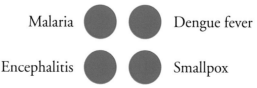 Dengue fever

Encephalitis Smallpox

Taking their titles from two of his signature phrases, *Wunnerful, Wunnerful!* and *Ah-One, Ah-Two!* were autobiographies of what bandleader?

Lawrence Welk   Nelson Riddle

Fred Waring   Guy Lombardo

Timothy Hutton won a 1980 Oscar for Best Supporting Actor for playing a troubled teen in what movie by first-time director Robert Redford?

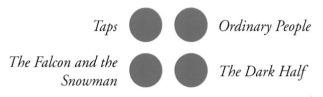

Taps   *Ordinary People*

The Falcon and the Snowman   *The Dark Half*

Husband-and-wife sociologists Robert and Helen Lynd wrote the 1929 book *Middletown: A Study in Contemporary American Culture* based on their studies of which midwestern city?

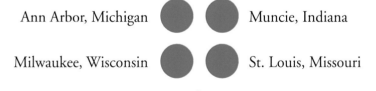

Ann Arbor, Michigan   Muncie, Indiana

Milwaukee, Wisconsin   St. Louis, Missouri

Which popular spring bird has the unfortunate genus name of *Turdus*?

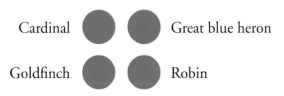

Cardinal   Great blue heron

Goldfinch   Robin

Which inventor came up with the first practical system for using alternating current, patenting the rotating magnetic field, the basis of most alternating-current machinery?

George Westinghouse  Thomas Edison

Nikola Tesla Alexander Graham Bell

How many human figures appear in the Grant Wood painting *American Gothic*?

1   6

2   13

Which type of triangle, by definition, has no two sides equal in length?

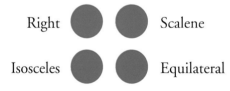

Right   Scalene

Isosceles   Equilateral

Which gas makes up 96% of the atmosphere of the planet Venus?

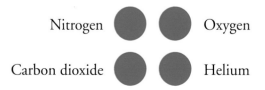

Nitrogen   Oxygen

Carbon dioxide   Helium

Who was the subject of paintings by Jacques-Louis David who is seen *Distributing the Eagles* and *In His Study at the Tuileries*?

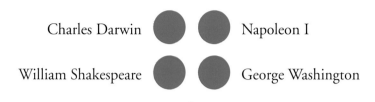

Charles Darwin ○ ○ Napoleon I

William Shakespeare ○ ○ George Washington

Tongass National Forest, the largest publicly owned forest in the United States, covers the panhandle of which U.S. state?

Oklahoma ○ ○ Missouri

Alaska ○ ○ Florida

The Gibson Desert, named for Alfred Gibson, an explorer who was lost there seeking water in the 1870s, is located in which country?

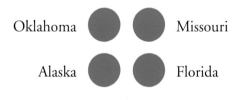

Abu Dhabi ○ ○ Australia

Mexico ○ ○ The Sudan

Which of these animals is not in the same genus as the cow?

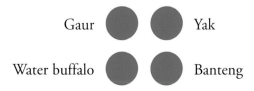

Gaur ○ ○ Yak

Water buffalo ○ ○ Banteng

The name of which star is derived from an Arabic term meaning "the left leg of the giant," referring to the figure of Orion?

Betelgeuse   Aldebaran

Rigel   Procyon

In 1881, which scientist perfected a way to isolate and weaken germs, developing vaccines against anthrax in sheep and cholera in chickens?

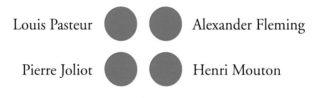

Louis Pasteur   Alexander Fleming

Pierre Joliot   Henri Mouton

Which city at the foot of the Sonoma Mountains was the site of the home and gardens of plant breeder Luther Burbank?

Glen Ellen   Sebastopol

Petaluma   Santa Rosa

Which director received Academy Awards for the human dramas *Mrs. Miniver* (1942) and *The Best Years of Our Lives* (1946)?

John Ford   Fred Zinnemann

William Wyler   George Stevens

Which asteroid approaches nearer the Sun than any other known body in the solar system except comets?

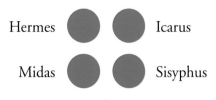

Hermes   Icarus

Midas   Sisyphus

Which of these radioactive heavy metals does not occur in nature?

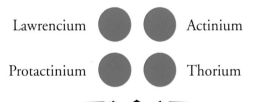

Lawrencium   Actinium

Protactinium   Thorium

In what effect are solids heated to high temperatures, so electrons can be emitted from the surface?

Lyman effect   Casimir effect

Venturi effect   Edison effect

Which element is second only to oxygen as the most abundant in the Earth's crust?

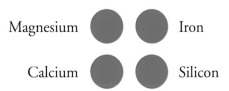

Magnesium   Iron

Calcium   Silicon

Besides man and other primates, what is the only animal that develops leprosy in nature?

Armadillo   Kangaroo

Hedgehog   Pangolin

What singer was the organizer and headliner of the phenomenally successful summer music festival Lilith Fair?

Tracy Chapman   Sarah McLachlan

Shawn Colvin   Paula Cole

Whose film career was launched with his appearance as a mentally disturbed choirboy alongside Richard Gere in the 1996 movie *Primal Fear*?

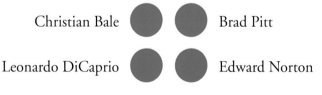

Christian Bale   Brad Pitt

Leonardo DiCaprio   Edward Norton

Which artist grew up in Sun Prairie, Wisconsin, but became famous for her desert landscapes of New Mexico?

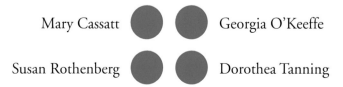

Mary Cassatt   Georgia O'Keeffe

Susan Rothenberg   Dorothea Tanning

What actor's numerical films include *The Whole Nine Yards*, *16 Blocks*, *The Fifth Element*, and *The Sixth Sense*?

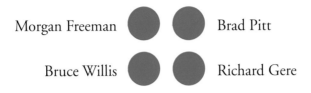

Morgan Freeman   Brad Pitt

Bruce Willis   Richard Gere

Who performed a tap dance on roller skates in the 1953 movie *I Love Melvin*?

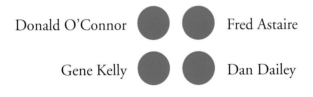

Donald O'Connor   Fred Astaire

Gene Kelly   Dan Dailey

What musical standard written by Hoagy Carmichael was an instrumental until fitted with lyrics by Mitchell Parrish in 1929?

"Mona Lisa"   "Stardust"

"Lazy River"   "Georgia on My Mind"

What was the name of the wisecracking housekeeper on *The Brady Bunch*?

Leslie   Hazel

Alice   Lynn

The ratio of the velocities of galaxies to their distances from Earth is the cosmological constant named after which astronomer?

Percival Lowell   Warren Offutt

Edwin Hubble   Scott Sheppard

Which actress played the mother of Charlton Heston in the biblical movies *The Ten Commandments* and *Ben-Hur*?

Marsha Hunt   Martha Scott

Pola Negri   Nina Foch

The last known specimens of the great auk were killed in June 1844 in which North Atlantic country?

Iceland   Spain

Scotland   Canada

The pleural cavity is located in which organ of the human body?

Stomach   Heart

Lungs   Pancreas

What country singer first gained national prominence when she won first prize on the CBS television show *Arthur Godfrey's Talent Scouts* for her performance of the song "Walkin' After Midnight"?

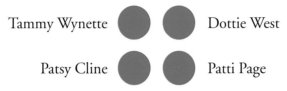

Tammy Wynette   Dottie West

Patsy Cline   Patti Page

Which gland is located alongside the trachea, or windpipe, in the neck?

Thyroid   Thymus

Pineal   Apocrine

Which disease is also known as infantile paralysis?

Polio   Rabies

Lockjaw   Hepatitis

The chamber trio of Isaac Stern on violin, Leonard Rose on cello, and Eugene Istomin on what instrument made recordings that came to be regarded as classics?

Flute   Viola

Harp   Piano

Luciano Pavarotti's last public appearance was in the opening ceremony of the 2006 Winter Olympics in Turin, Italy, where he sang his signature aria, "Nessun dorma," from which opera?

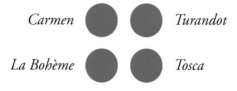

Carmen *Turandot*

La Bohème *Tosca*

In January 2007 *Down Beat* magazine featured Brad Mehldau, characterizing him as perhaps the most influential jazz artist of his generation. Which musical instrument does Mehldau play?

Saxophone Piano

Guitar Bass

What does the A stand for in AM radio?

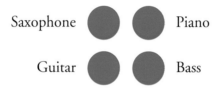

Amplitude Alternating

Audio Adjusted

Members of which 1960s rock band included Nico, John Cale, and Lou Reed?

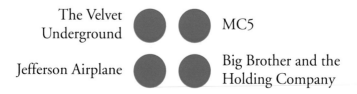

The Velvet Underground MC5

Jefferson Airplane Big Brother and the Holding Company

What South African–born British nun appeared on a series of television shows to popularize art and wrote a number of books as an art critic?

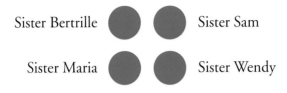

Sister Bertrille   Sister Sam

Sister Maria   Sister Wendy

What unit of force is equal to the force of 100,000 dynes?

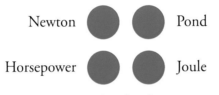

Newton   Pond

Horsepower   Joule

On which building are you most likely to find a flèche?

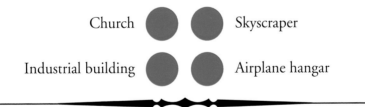

Church   Skyscraper

Industrial building   Airplane hangar

In Japan, which poisonous fish is served as fugu and must be carefully cleaned and prepared by a specially trained chef?

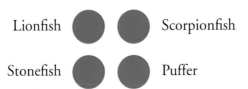

Lionfish   Scorpionfish

Stonefish   Puffer

A dormer window is typically used to illuminate which room of the house?

Kitchen   Bedroom

Basement   Living room

The length of a degree of arc of latitude on the Earth's surface is approximately how many miles?

7   700

70   7,000

The diamond shape of the central emblem on the flag of which U.S. state symbolizes the state's diamond production, the only state with a diamond mine?

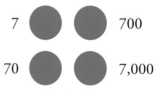

Arkansas   Mississippi

Minnesota   Alabama

Which type of poisonous substance is found in the pit of the wild cherry and apple seeds?

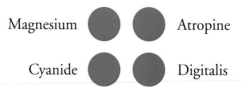

Magnesium   Atropine

Cyanide   Digitalis

The natural food of the silkworm is the leaves of which plant?

Quince ● ● Hollyhock

Eucalyptus ● ● Mulberry

On which of these islands are you most likely to find a bird-of-paradise?

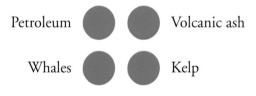

New Guinea ● ● Easter Island

Prince Edward Island ● ● Tahiti

What is the source of ambergris, a waxy, fragrant substance used in some perfumes?

Petroleum ● ● Volcanic ash

Whales ● ● Kelp

Valentina Tereshkova was the first female Russian cosmonaut in space in 1963. In what year did Sally Ride become the first American woman in space?

1973 ● ● 1978

1976 ● ● 1983

The Java man fossils discovered in the 1890s were the first known fossils of which human ancestor?

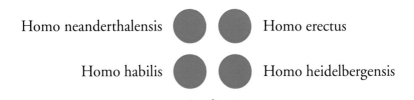

Homo neanderthalensis   Homo erectus

Homo habilis   Homo heidelbergensis

Which movie featured the ensemble cast of Kevin Kline, John Cleese, Michael Palin, and Jamie Lee Curtis?

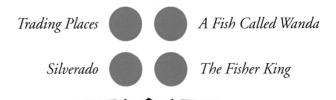

Trading Places   *A Fish Called Wanda*

Silverado   *The Fisher King*

Which part of the human body would be subject to the surgical procedure known as a radial keratotomy?

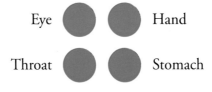

Eye   Hand

Throat   Stomach

Somatotropin, a peptide hormone found in the human body, is also known as GH. What does the G stand for?

Gamma   Greek

Granular   Growth

The Shoemaker-Levy 9 comet crashed into which planet in 1994?

Jupiter   Uranus

Saturn   Neptune

Which country singer had a crossover pop hit in 1963 with "The End of the World"?

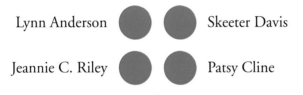

Lynn Anderson   Skeeter Davis

Jeannie C. Riley   Patsy Cline

In which month does the Perseid meteor shower occur annually?

August   October

May   January

What surname was used by both members of the White Stripes, Jack and Meg?

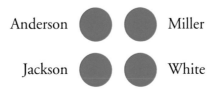

Anderson   Miller

Jackson   White

How many legs does a horseshoe crab have?

6   12

8   16

Which British rock musician debuted with the punk-influenced album *My Aim Is True*, going on later in his career to collaborate with the very un-punk Burt Bacharach?

Graham Parker   Elvis Costello

Joe Jackson   Ian Dury

Which artist mastered the difficult art of stained glass in the late 1950s, and designed windows at locations such as the United Nations building in New York (1964) and the Art Institute of Chicago (1977)?

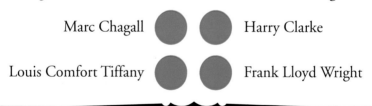

Marc Chagall   Harry Clarke

Louis Comfort Tiffany   Frank Lloyd Wright

What triangular gable forming the end of the roof slope over a portico was the crowning feature of the Greek temple front?

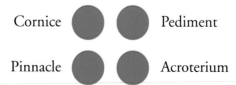

Cornice   Pediment

Pinnacle   Acroterium

Which of these painters was *not* born in France?

Edgar Degas 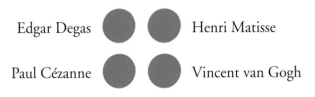 Henri Matisse

Paul Cézanne Vincent van Gogh

The Freer Gallery of Art and the Corcoran Gallery of Art are both located in which city?

Denver 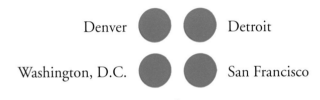 Detroit

Washington, D.C. San Francisco

A noted 1893 opera by Engelbert Humperdinck was based on which folktale made familiar by the brothers Grimm?

"Hansel and Gretel" 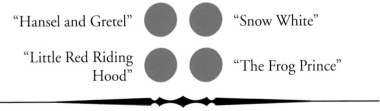 "Snow White"

"Little Red Riding Hood" "The Frog Prince"

Which French painter's most impressive candlelit scenes are *The Newborn*, *St. Joseph the Carpenter*, and *The Lamentation Over St. Sebastian*?

Camille Pissarro 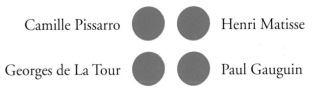 Henri Matisse

Georges de La Tour Paul Gauguin

What was the surname of the nobleman and Italian physicist whose invention of the electric battery provided the first source of continuous current?

Tesla   Volta

Joule   Torricelli

Which artist, who was ill much of the last 13 years of his life, designed the magnificent Chapelle du Rosaire at Vence as a gift to the Dominican nuns who cared for him?

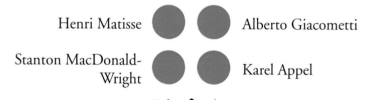

Henri Matisse   Alberto Giacometti

Stanton MacDonald-Wright   Karel Appel

Between 1971 and 1985, which artist secretly painted Helga Testorf, his neighbor in Chadds Ford, Pennsylvania, creating hundreds of images of her, including nudes?

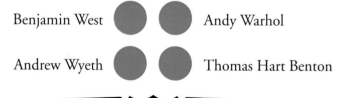

Benjamin West   Andy Warhol

Andrew Wyeth   Thomas Hart Benton

What astronomer was the narrator of the 1980 TV series *Cosmos*?

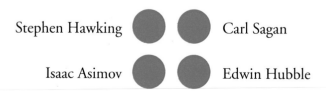

Stephen Hawking   Carl Sagan

Isaac Asimov   Edwin Hubble

Before he legally changed his first name to Buzz, what was the first name of Apollo 11 astronaut "Buzz" Aldrin?

Donald   Edwin

John   Michael

How many atoms of oxygen are in a molecule of sulfuric acid?

1   3

2   4

Which portion of the brain accounts for two-thirds of its total weight?

Cerebrum   Hippocampus

Cerebellum   Forebrain

The fruit of which tree in the hibiscus family has a pungent odor that has been compared to that of Limburger cheese?

Mango   Sapodilla

Durian   Pawpaw

Which drug was developed in 1913 as an appetite suppressant known as MDMA?

Ecstasy   Heroin

OxyContin   Methadone

In which James Bond film did Dame Judi Dench take over the role of M?

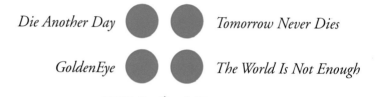

Die Another Day   *Tomorrow Never Dies*

GoldenEye   *The World Is Not Enough*

Which movie won the first Oscar for Best Animated Feature?

The Lion King   *Finding Nemo*

The Incredibles   *Shrek*

Frau Adele Bloch-Bauer was sold to the Neue Galerie in New York City in 2006 for a then-record price of $135 million. Who was the artist?

Vincent van Gogh   Gustav Klimt

Anthony van Dyck   Peter Paul Rubens

Which bird, believed to be extinct in the United States since the mid-1950s, was announced by a team of researchers in 2005 to have been rediscovered in Arkansas?

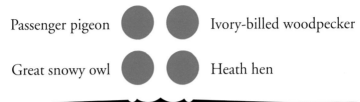

Passenger pigeon   Ivory-billed woodpecker

Great snowy owl   Heath hen

Members of which group of artists founded in Moscow in 1909, and named after a playing card, were for the next few years the leading exponents of avant-garde art in Russia?

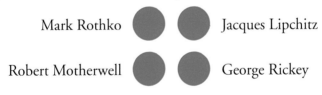

Jack of Diamonds   Eight of Hearts

Ace of Spades   Joker

From 1958 to 1966 which artist worked intermittently on a series of 14 immense canvases eventually placed in a nondenominational chapel in Houston, Texas, that was posthumously renamed after him?

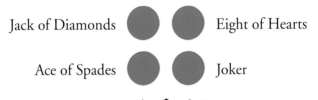

Mark Rothko   Jacques Lipchitz

Robert Motherwell   George Rickey

Which Japanese architect, known for his minimalist concrete buildings, designed the Azuma House (1975–76) in Osaka and the Koshino House (1979–81) in Ashiya?

Kenzo Tange   Fumihiko Maki

Hiroshi Hara   Ando Tadao

Which innovative composer wrote the *Poème électronique* for the Philips Pavilion at the Brussels World's Fair in 1958, for which the sound was intended to be distributed by 425 loudspeakers?

Arthur Honegger 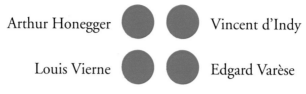 Vincent d'Indy

Louis Vierne Edgard Varèse

Bluish-white specks called Koplik spots appear in the mouth 24 to 36 hours before the outbreak of which disease?

Scarlet fever  Malaria

Measles Rheumatic fever

Which composer's only full-length opera, *The Rake's Progress*, was a Neoclassical work with a libretto by W.H. Auden and the American writer Chester Kallman?

Pyotr Ilyich Tchaikovsky 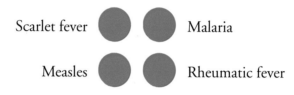 Modest Mussorgsky

Aleksander Borodin Igor Stravinsky

Which portion of the brain serves as a pathway for nerve fibers connecting the cerebral cortex with the cerebellum?

Pons  Pia mater

Hypothalamus Medulla oblongata

The smooth, slow circling of a spinning top is precession; the uneven wobbling of the top is called what?

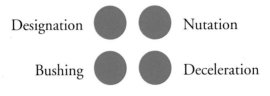

Designation

Nutation

Bushing

Deceleration

John Frederick Kensett, Fitz Hugh Lane, and Martin Johnson Heade were important painters using what style emphasizing a unique clarity of light?

Stuckism

Luminism

Chiaroscuro

Chromism

What artist who experimented with the comic strip as an art theme was the first American artist to exhibit at London's Tate Gallery in 1966?

Claes Oldenburg

Tom Wesselmann

James Rosenquist

Roy Lichtenstein

Which Mexican artist painted a series of watercolors dealing with the lives of prostitutes that was collectively titled *House of Tears*?

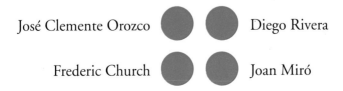

José Clemente Orozco

Diego Rivera

Frederic Church

Joan Miró

The works of which Surrealist artist included a fish with human legs, a man with a bird cage for a torso, and a gentleman leaning over a wall beside his pet lion?

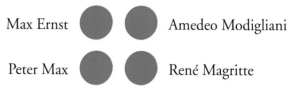

Max Ernst   Amedeo Modigliani

Peter Max   René Magritte

Roentgenium has the highest atomic number of known elements on the periodic table. What is roentgenium's atomic number?

104   111

107   116

SCSI (pronounced "scuzzy") was once a common standard for connecting peripheral devices to desktop computers. What does the first "S" in SCSI stand for?

Standard   Syncopated

Small   Serial

Edward Hopper's most famous painting, showing a diner, shares its title with what Sylvester Stallone movie?

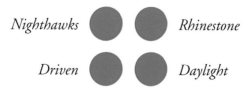

Nighthawks   *Rhinestone*

Driven   *Daylight*

How many elements on the periodic table are identified by a single letter?

10   14

13   19

Which popular cartoon character was created by Otto Messmer?

Popeye   Felix the Cat

Woody Woodpecker   Mighty Mouse

The Messenger spacecraft was launched in 2004 to study the surface of which planet?

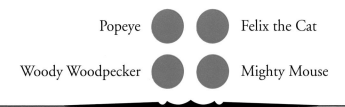

Mercury   Uranus

Saturn   Neptune

Lightning rods are typically made of what conductive metal?

Iron   Nickel

Copper   Silver

From 1969 to 1991, Sir Georg Solti was the music director for which American city's symphony orchestra?

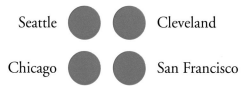

Seattle   Cleveland

Chicago   San Francisco

Sir John Cockcroft and Ernest Walton were awarded the Nobel Prize for Physics in 1951 for pioneering the use of which device?

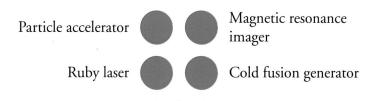

Particle accelerator   Magnetic resonance imager

Ruby laser   Cold fusion generator

For a constant force in physics, what is equal to the magnitude of the force (F) times the displacement (d) of an object?

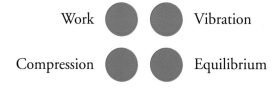

Work   Vibration

Compression   Equilibrium

Which metallic element was first isolated in 1783 by the Spanish chemist Fausto Elhuyar in partnership with his brother Juan José Elhuyar?

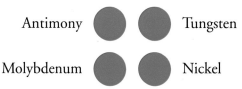

Antimony   Tungsten

Molybdenum   Nickel

In its pure state, what color is cholesterol?

White  Yellow

Pink Black

Which Russian composer was also a scientist notable for his research on aldehydes?

Mikhail Glinka  Nikolay Rimsky-Korsakov

Aleksandr Dargomyzhsky Aleksandr Borodin

What Italian philosopher, astronomer, and proponent of heliocentrism was excommunicated from both Catholic and Protestant churches, and later burned at the stake in a public square in Rome for his beliefs?

Pietro Pomponazzi  Lucilio Vanini

Alessandro Achillini Giordano Bruno

During the 1960s, which conductor was simultaneously the musical director of the Montreal Symphony and the Los Angeles Philharmonic?

Daniel Barenboim 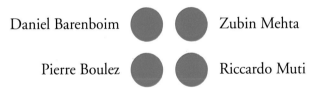 Zubin Mehta

Pierre Boulez Riccardo Muti

When light passes through the eye, it is focused into an image on what layer of tissue?

Retina  Iris

Uvea Cornea

Philately refers to the collection of which items?

Vinyl records 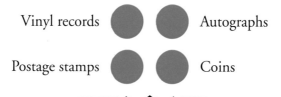 Autographs

Postage stamps Coins

Which Flemish painter was appointed court painter by Charles I of England in 1632 and knighted the same year?

Anthony van Dyck 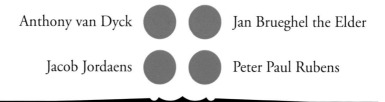 Jan Brueghel the Elder

Jacob Jordaens Peter Paul Rubens

Which flying vehicle gets its name from the French word for "steer"?

Blimp  Helicopter

Dirigible Zeppelin

English physician John Snow discovered in the 1850s that which disease was waterborne?

Tetanus   Cholera

Typhoid   Diphtheria

Which substance is the principal form in which carbohydrates are stored in higher animals, occurring primarily in the liver and muscles?

Ketose   Heparin

Glycogen   Cellulose

Art patron Peggy Guggenheim married what artist in 1941?

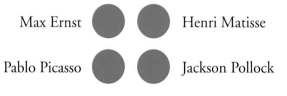

Max Ernst   Henri Matisse

Pablo Picasso   Jackson Pollock

Dora Maar and Marie-Thérèse Walter, referred to as the "Weeping Women" in a 1994 art exhibition, were muses (and mistresses) of what painter?

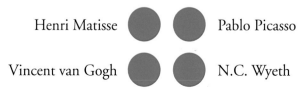

Henri Matisse   Pablo Picasso

Vincent van Gogh   N.C. Wyeth

Whose *Symphony No. 8 in E Flat Major* for eight soloists, double choir, and orchestra is known as the "Symphony of a Thousand," owing to the large forces it requires?

Gustav Mahler ⬤ ⬤ Richard Strauss

Johannes Brahms ⬤ ⬤ Gustav Holst

Which French artist famously painted ten variations of the Mont Sainte-Victoire?

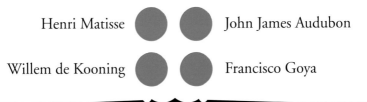

Pierre-Auguste Renoir ⬤ ⬤ Paul Cézanne

Claude Monet ⬤ ⬤ Marcel Duchamp

Hilary Spurling won the 2005 Whitbread Book of the Year Award for the second volume of her biography of what artist?

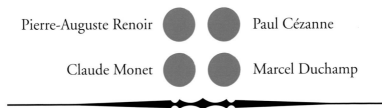

Henri Matisse ⬤ ⬤ John James Audubon

Willem de Kooning ⬤ ⬤ Francisco Goya

In the human body, what is the main product of the parotid gland?

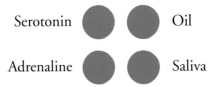

Serotonin ⬤ ⬤ Oil

Adrenaline ⬤ ⬤ Saliva

Which chemical element is named after the Norse goddess of beauty?

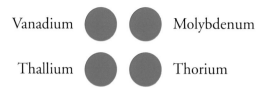

Vanadium　　　Molybdenum

Thallium　　　Thorium

Which of these creatures belongs to the phylum Platyhelminthes?

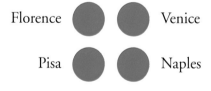

Ferret　　　Flea

Flatworm　　　Frog

The artistic Bellini family played a dominant role in the art of what Italian city?

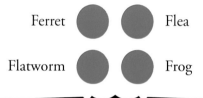

Florence　　　Venice

Pisa　　　Naples

Which 1957 movie western was remade by director James Mangold in 2007?

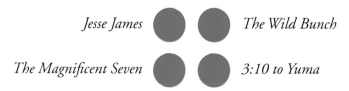

Jesse James　　　*The Wild Bunch*

The Magnificent Seven　　　*3:10 to Yuma*

The Great Imambara and the Rumi Darwaza (Turkish Gate) are architectural treasures of what city in India?

Mumbai   Lucknow

Pune   Calcutta

Pellagra is a nutritional disorder caused by the deficiency of what vitamin?

Vitamin K   Niacin

Riboflavin   Vitamin C

Which peer-to-peer file sharing computer program was created by Shawn Fanning in 1999?

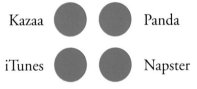

Kazaa   Panda

iTunes   Napster

Sir Arthur Evans and Heinrich Schliemann are important names in what science?

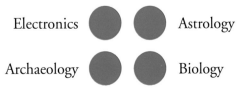

Electronics   Astrology

Archaeology   Biology

Who designed the innovative Guggenheim Museum building in New York City, built in 1959?

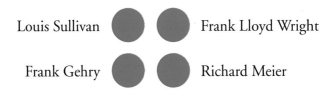

Louis Sullivan   Frank Lloyd Wright

Frank Gehry   Richard Meier

Which artist first became prominent as the principal advertiser of the actress Sarah Bernhardt in Paris, designing posters for several theatrical productions featuring Bernhardt (and sets and costumes for her as well)?

Paul Gauguin   Aubrey Beardsley

Alphonse Mucha   Henri de Toulouse-Lautrec

What former railroad worker and Country Music Hall of Fame member was nicknamed "The Singing Brakeman"?

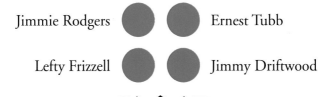

Jimmie Rodgers   Ernest Tubb

Lefty Frizzell   Jimmy Driftwood

Which film comedian, who always claimed to hate Christmas, died on December 25, 1946?

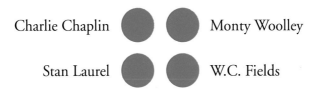

Charlie Chaplin   Monty Woolley

Stan Laurel   W.C. Fields

Collier's Weekly paid what artist $50,000, said at the time to be the largest fee ever paid to an illustrator, for a two-page illustration every week for a year, usually of comic or sentimental situations of the day?

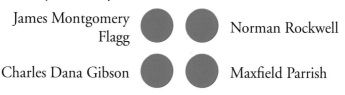

James Montgomery Flagg   Norman Rockwell

Charles Dana Gibson   Maxfield Parrish

At the Salon of 1884, which artist showed what is probably his best-known picture (regarded at the time as eccentric and erotic), *Madame X*, a portrait of Madame Gautreau, a famous Parisian beauty?

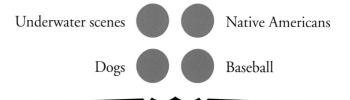

Diego Velázquez   Winslow Homer

J.M.W. Turner   John Singer Sargent

For what subject matter was American artist George Catlin famous?

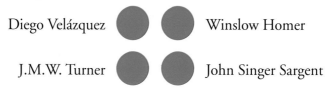

Underwater scenes   Native Americans

Dogs   Baseball

Sb is the symbol for which chemical element?

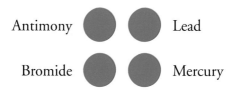

Antimony   Lead

Bromide   Mercury

What is the surname of the father and son awarded the Nobel Prize in Physics in 1915 for their study of crystal structures?

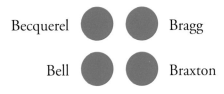

Becquerel   Bragg

Bell   Braxton

What is the name of the whiskerlike organs near the mouth of a fish that help it locate food?

Wattles   Gudgeon

Tenches   Barbels

Patrick Steptoe and Robert Edwards perfected in vitro fertilization of the human egg. Their technique made possible the birth of Louise Brown, the world's first "test-tube baby," born in which year?

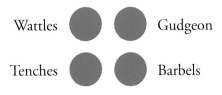

1976   1980

1978   1982

In 2002 nearly half the U.S. states changed their laws so that which vehicle could be legally ridden on sidewalks and cycle paths?

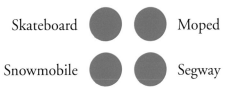

Skateboard   Moped

Snowmobile   Segway

What were the first names of the Mayo brothers who founded the Mayo Clinic in Rochester, Minnesota?

Lance and Neil   Christopher and John

Thomas and August   William and Charles

Which of the following animals is *not* a marsupial?

Tasmanian devil   Ring-tailed lemur

Bandicoot   Opossum

Hablot Knight Browne, the best-known illustrator of books by Charles Dickens, signed his work with what pseudonym?

Boz   Omar

Phiz   Punch

Which British architect, who worked in the style of High Victorian medieval eclecticism, designed the Natural History Museum in London?

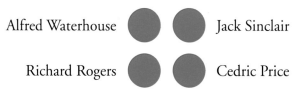

Alfred Waterhouse   Jack Sinclair

Richard Rogers   Cedric Price

Which method of painting evolved by Paul Gauguin, Émile Bernard, and Louis Anquetin in the 1880s to emphasize two-dimensional flat patterns, thus breaking with Impressionist art and theory?

Fauvism   Synthetism

Cubism   Luminism

Which British writer, known for his belief in spiritualism and fairies, was considered as a possible perpetrator of the Piltdown man hoax of 1912?

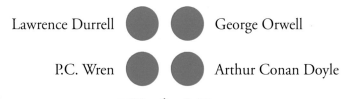

Lawrence Durrell   George Orwell

P.C. Wren   Arthur Conan Doyle

The integral part of a common logarithm is called the characteristic. What is the decimal part known as?

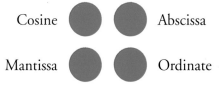

Cosine   Abscissa

Mantissa   Ordinate

Which actor also starred in the only film he ever directed, the 1961 western *One-Eyed Jacks*?

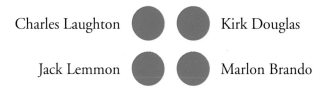

Charles Laughton   Kirk Douglas

Jack Lemmon   Marlon Brando

Which Jean-Luc Godard film, about a petty crook who admires Humphrey Bogart, jarred 1950s audiences with hand-held camera work and jagged editing?

Breathless   *Contempt*

Made in U.S.A.   *The Razor's Edge*

In 1911, which composer wrote his only opera, *Duke Bluebeard's Castle*, an allegorical treatment of the legendary wife-murderer with a score permeated by characteristics of traditional Hungarian folk songs?

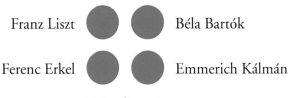

Franz Liszt   Béla Bartók

Ferenc Erkel   Emmerich Kálmán

What composer and cello virtuoso helped found the American Society of Composers, Authors, and Publishers (ASCAP) in 1914?

Victor Herbert   Meredith Willson

Rudolf Friml   Pablo Casals

Who was the subject of Jules Massenet's final opera, written in 1910?

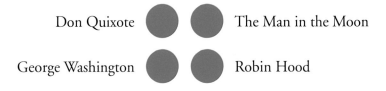

Don Quixote   The Man in the Moon

George Washington   Robin Hood

Which opera was presented as the opening performance for the Metropolitan Opera in New York City in 1883?

Aida   *Otello*

Faust   *La Bohème*

Who put words to the music of Andrew Lloyd Webber for the rock opera *Jesus Christ Superstar*?

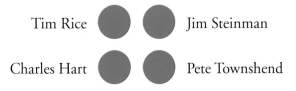

Tim Rice   Jim Steinman

Charles Hart   Pete Townshend

Which Japanese conceptual artist created more than 2,000 paintings in his *Today* (or *Date*) series in more than 100 cities around the world?

Jun Tagami   On Kawara

Kaoru Kawano   Masaki Fujihata

Eugène Atget, Man Ray, and Henri Cartier-Bresson used which medium for their art?

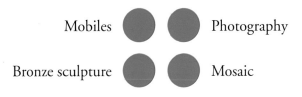

Mobiles   Photography

Bronze sculpture   Mosaic

Whose sculpture *Bird in Space* was the cause of a two-year court battle beginning in 1926, due to U.S. customs believing that it was an industrial part and not a work of art?

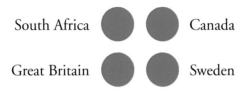

Marta Pan   Jacques Lipchitz

Constantin Brancusi   Alexander Calder

The first human heart transplant was performed by surgeon Christiaan Barnard in 1967 in which country?

South Africa   Canada

Great Britain   Sweden

In which ocean does the major Benguela Current flow, as a branch of the West Wind Drift?

Atlantic   Indian

Arctic   Pacific

Which analytic chemistry technique involves separating a liquid or gas into its component parts?

Microprinting   Solvent extraction

RNA interference   Chromatography

For which disease did German scientist Robert Koch isolate the bacillus responsible, receiving the Nobel Prize for Physiology or Medicine in 1905?

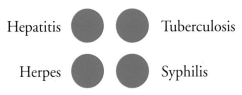

Hepatitis   Tuberculosis

Herpes   Syphilis

What father of modern chaos theory introduced the "butterfly effect" metaphor: the flapping of a butterfly's wings in China today may cause a tornado in Kansas tomorrow?

Edward Lorenz   George Crile

Linus Pauling   Sir John Eccles

Scientists found evidence of which chemical element in spectrographs of the Sun in 1868, but did not find it on Earth until a discovery by British chemist Sir William Ramsay in 1895?

Mercury   Plutonium

Uranium   Helium

What is the subject of the science of pedology?

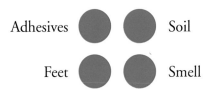

Adhesives   Soil

Feet   Smell

Which acid was referred to as "oil of vitriol"?

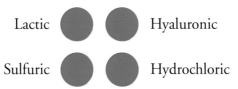

Lactic   Hyaluronic

Sulfuric   Hydrochloric

Which 19th-century scientist belonged to a small Christian sect called the Sandemanians?

Michael Faraday   Gregor Mendel

Charles Darwin   Louis Pasteur

Which eminent scientist once worked as an obscure clerk for the Swiss patent office?

Niels Bohr   Albert Einstein

Enrico Fermi   Stephen Hawking

According to the old medical theory of the four humors, melancholy was caused by an imbalance in which of the humors?

Yellow bile   Blood

Black bile   Phlegm

Karl von Frisch shared a 1973 Nobel Prize in Physiology or Medicine for his study of communication among which insects?

Butterflies   Ladybugs

Ants   Bees

Because it has no stable or long-lived isotopes, which chemical element was given its name from the Greek word meaning "unstable"?

Hafnium   Lutetium

Astatine   Actinium

Which writer established himself as a major author with his first two published novels, the satires *Crome Yellow* (1921) and *Antic Hay* (1923)?

P.G. Wodehouse   William Dean Howells

Frank Norris   Aldous Huxley

What hero of myth used arrows dipped in the poisonous blood of the Hydra, eventually leading to his own accidental death by the poison at his wife's hands, according to Sophocles' tragedy *Trachinian Women*?

Hercules   Theseus

Apollo   Cupid

Which actor starred on the TV shows *The Courtship of Eddie's Father*, *My Favorite Martian*, and *The Incredible Hulk*?

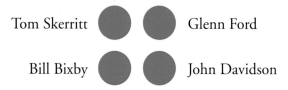

Tom Skerritt   Glenn Ford

Bill Bixby   John Davidson

From his study of valence, Richard Abegg concluded that for the most stable configuration, the number of electrons in the outer group of an atom is what number, occurring in all the noble gases except helium?

3   8

6   10

Film executive Irving Thalberg was "the boy wonder of Hollywood" while serving as the production manager for what Hollywood studio in the 1930s?

Columbia   RKO

MGM   Universal

Critics in India charged that passages dealing with sex in the 1997 novel *The God of Small Things* were obscene, leading what author to declare she might never write another book (but she did)?

Jhumpa Lahiri   Arundhati Roy

Madhur Jaffrey   Rimi B. Chatterjee